DISABILITY IN MODERN CHILDREN'S FICTION

Disability in Modern Children's Fiction

JOHN QUICKE

CROOM HELM
London & Sydney

BROOKLINE BOOKS
29 Ware Street
Cambridge, MA 02138
(617) 868-0360

© 1985 John Quicke
Croom Helm Ltd, Provident House, Burrell Row,
Beckenham, Kent BR3 1AT
Croom Helm Australia Pty Ltd, First Floor, 139 King Street,
Sydney, NSW 2001, Australia

British Library Cataloguing in Publication Data

Quicke, John
    Disability in modern children's fiction.
    1. Children's stories, English – History
    and criticism. 2. Handicapped in literature
    I. Title
    823'.914'093520816   PR888.C5/
    ISBN 0-7099-2102-0

Published in the USA and dependencies,
Central and South America by
Brookline Books, 29 Ware Street,
Cambridge, Massachusetts 02138

Library of Congress Cataloging in Publication Data

Quicke, John, 1941–
    Disability in modern children's fiction.

    Bibliography: p.
    Includes index.
    1. Children's stories, English – History and criti-
cism. 2. Handicapped in literature. I. Title.
PR888.C5Q53   1985   823'.914'093520816   84-19844
ISBN 0-914797-09-3

Typeset by Mayhew Typesetting, Bristol, UK
Printed and bound in Great Britain

CONTENTS

PREFACE

This book is being published concurrently for British and American Readers. Written by a British author, the text contains many expressions particular to Great Britain, and the practices common there. The meaning of many of these expressions can be determined from their context. Others are explained in the glossary at the back of the book. This glossary includes a description of the educational system in Great Britain and some salient features of the system for providing services to disabled children.

Two concepts bear explaining since they are frequently mentioned in the book's discussions. The Warnock Committee was appointed to consider the educational needs of handicapped children and young people. It has been one of the most important influences on special educational policy and practice in Great Britain during the late 1970s and early 1980s and its report is the document to which nearly all local education authorities refer when they wish to find guidance, support and justification for their actions and plans.

An important recommendation which this committee made was that, if at all possible, students with special educational needs should attend ordinary schools.

This is reflected in the strong emphasis on an integrationist philosophy espoused in this book. For American readers, this same emphasis is embodied in the Federal law, Public Law 94-142, The Education of All Handicapped Children Act. This law also requires that handicapped children be educated in the least restrictive setting. What may be confusing to American readers is a terminological issue: the term 'integration' refers to the education of black and white children, or racial integration. The term 'mainstreaming' has been applied to these practices with children having special educational needs.

ACKNOWLEDGEMENTS

I should like to offer my thanks to Frank and Winifred Whitehead for their support, encouragement and helpful comments on the first draft of the manuscript; to Gaynor Eyre of the Sheffield Schools Library Service for her invaluable assistance in finding and obtaining the relevant children's literature; to Patricia Kluczewski and Oliver, for the information they provided about a young child's reaction to quasi-fiction; to Anita Fletcher, Carole Overall, Louise Walmsley and Anne Quicke for their careful typing of the manuscript.

Acknowledgements are also due to Nigel Snell and Hamish Hamilton Ltd for permission to reproduce material from the book *Jane Has Asthma*; likewise to Paul White and Adam and Charles Black for permission to include material from *Janet at School*; and to Maureen Galvani and Dinosaur, for permission to include material from *I Have Diabetes* and *I Use a Wheelchair*. The illustrations taken from *Rachel, The Boy Who Couldn't Hear* and *Mike* by Michael Charlton are reproduced by permission of The Bodley Head.

1 INTRODUCTION

The inspiration for this book derived from two sources: first, the author's concern with the implementation of integrationist policies for those children defined under the auspices of the Education Act 1981 as having special educational needs; and the second, his interest in fiction as a means of developing social awareness and emotional sensitivity amongst all children and young people. To a large extent the successful integration of children with special educational needs depends on their acceptance by 'normal' peers in the ordinary school. As the Jount Council for the Education of Handicapped Children observed in their 1980 Report: 'Integration also requires acceptance by the majority when it affects them personally'. They go on to suggest that not to take this dimension into account is tantamount to a dereliction of duty on the part of teachers: 'Headteachers and staffs in ordinary schools have as their foremost duty the fulfilment of the needs of the majority'.

The concern of these authors stems partly from a belief, widespread amongst advocates of segregated provision, that the normal classroom is a somewhat inhospitable place for the child with a disability or difficulty. This belief, often these days grounded in a prejudice against the comprehensive school, is based on the assumption that children with special educational needs need to be protected from the boisterousness or insensitivity or faulty attitudes of their 'normal' peers. The latter, it is felt, may even resent 'special' children for taking up too much of the teacher's time.

Whilst accepting that the ordinary school is not a bed of roses, supporters of integration have been prepared to risk placements in the mainstream of ordinary school because they feel there is an even greater risk of stigma and lowered achievement in a special placement. They also point to the fact that there is little unequivocal 'objective' evidence of the effectiveness of special education (see Tomlinson 1981; Galloway and Goodwin 1979). More importantly, however, it is felt that an optimistic view should be taken of the capacities of 'normal' children to befriend and welcome 'special needs' children, and of their ability to accept that some form of positive discrimination will be required for them; a view which this author strongly supports.

1

However, to take an optimistic view is not to be naïve about the realities of children's interpersonal relationships in classroom and playground. Although teasing and bullying of children with special educational needs may be rare (see Hegarty and Pocklington, 1981, p. 463), this does not meant that one can be complacent about the pervasiveness of positive peer attitudes and behaviour. Children's views reflect those of the culture in which they are located, and although we like to think that ours is an enlightened culture there is still a good deal of discrimination and prejudice against children with disabilities or difficulties, often unrecognised as such because it is institutionalised and taken for granted. Rather than adopting a romantic attitude about the 'natural' goodness of children, a more realistic view is to assume that attitudes towards disability and difficulty will be as diverse amongst children as they are in society generally.

I think even supporters of integration have to accept that genuine comprehensivisation is a reform which has been only partially implemented. Most schools still tend to be competitive and hierarchically organised, and this in itself militates against the development of a positive and co-operative attitude towards children with special needs. Discrimination against such children works through the formal curriculum by providing them with an unnecessarily impoverished diet, and through the hidden curriculum (see Hargreaves, 1982, Ch. 1) by conveying messages about their inferior or separate status. Not all schools are equally inhospitable for the child with special needs, and not all children have imbibed the competitive ethos, but it is true of many.

Competitiveness in schools creates divisions between children based on their relative positions in the rat race (see Henry, 1963). Even peer cultures designed to provide dignity and identity for those who opt out are often not open to 'special needs' children. It is not that many children, any more than many teachers, are conscious of discriminatory behaviour (in fact, most would probably deny it), but they are often too preoccupied with their own advancement or lack of it or, if they are indifferent or opposed to official school values, with survival strategies (see Woods, 1980) or cultural oppositional activities (see Willis, 1977) to be concerned with the problems of their peers with special needs.

In the wider society there are other influences at work. Although ours claims to be an age of realism and progressive policies, there are, latent to the dominant culture, ideas about handicap and disability from an earlier period which still have considerable force. An example is the notion, which runs through the history of Western civilisation and is legitimated by various religious teachings, that disability indicates possession by the devil or by an evil force, or is the outcome of evil doing. In ancient Greece and Rome disabilities were regarded as punishment from the gods and this was used to justify a eugenics policy which in Rome, for example, led to mentally defective persons being prevented from marrying. During the medieval period the ambivalence of Christianity towards disabled people was reflected in beliefs about their either being related to Satan or as being 'sacred beings' — innocents unstained by normal and sinful human characteristics. Luther was of the opinion that changelings had no soul, and advocated that children so afflicted should be taken to the river and drowned. The link between disability and evil is even present in the Victorian period, albeit in a somewhat different form — not implanted so much as the outcome of immoral behaviour — as well as the alternative association between disablement and highly virtuous and loving behaviour. 'Miracle' cures occurred as the result of good works and good thoughts coupled with a degree of silent suffering and self-denial.

There are other hangovers from the past which still influence our perceptions. The notion of disabled people being non-human, and more like animals or vegetables is illustrated in the following quotations from Shearer (1981):

It was in 1884 that a mental-retardation worker characterized one of his charges like this: 'With great, soft, jet eyes, he reminds one of a seal.' The mental-retardation worker who said: 'A lot of them can't talk, the same as animals can't; I've always said that what we need here is a vet, not a psychiatrist,' was talking at the beginning of the 1970s. It is no uncommon to hear the words of mental institutions which house the most disabled residents spoken of as 'farmyards', places where you need to 'take your bucket and shovel'. (p. 82)

In the spastics ward, six-year-old Shirley played with her tears, whirling her fingers disconsolately round in them as they puddled on the bare table in front of her. Her actions epitomized a bleak existence. One of the visitors said, 'These children are cabbages' and the others agreed with him, but perhaps it had not occurred to them to look at Shirley and consider that cabbages don't cry. (p. 83)

Such ideas are some amongst many of this ilk that contemporary society has inherited. It would be pleasant to think that they were being gradually expunged as our society progressed to a more desirable state, but there is nothing inevitable about this occurrence (see Booth, Potts and Swann, 1982, p. 7). In fact, one could argue that it is just as likely that as far as children with special needs are concerned things could get worse. For example, there are signs that the present anti-Welfare State, self-help ideology is beginning to work its way into the consciousness of young people. As Angela Neustatter writes, quoting anthropologist Ted Polhemus:

> The kids are tuned into the idea that it is a mercenary, self-seeking society where you help yourself and tough for those who go under. Now part of that is, of course, looking as though you belong to the *status quo*, that you are not unemployed or in any way disadvantaged. Of course, the idea of a sleek, orderly youth will appeal to some but the other side is that this new image is a far less *caring attitude* to others (*Times Educational Supplement*, 29.7.83, p. 15)

This, of course, is only the briefest of overviews of cultural features which are working against the integration of pupils with special needs. My contention is that such ideas are pervasive even if they are not overtly stated – they are latent to the consciousness of many children and adults in our society. In my view there is enough evidence here to justify a teaching intervention which tackles the problem directly by including a planned element in the curriculum specifically designed to encourage positive attitudes and action towards peers with special needs, just as there is a case for curricula to foster racial tolerance and awareness of gender issues.

If it is agreed that some curriculum innovation is necessary, there is still the question of what is the best way to deal with the topic. Many teachers feel that the most fruitful approach is to tackle prejudice in the setting in which it is spontaneously articulated, i.e. when incidents occur involving pupils with special needs. This can be planned up to a point (or more accurately the teacher's reaction can be planned), and it is part of a curriculum broadly interpreted to include informal as well as formal elements. A more formal approach would be the inclusion of special needs as one of a number of topics to be discussed in the class group. A brief, unpublished survey carried out by the author in a northern city suggested that a range of formal approaches were being employed by teachers in secondary schools. The most popular was to introduce lesson content on the topic of 'disabilities', which might involve material from novels where the central character had some form of special need, or factual material in the context of a discussion about social policies. Less popular were visits to hospitals, training centres and other establishments catering for disabled people and visits to the school from various charitable bodies or disabled adults themselves. Such visits to out of school locations were sometimes part of a community-service project.

This brings me to the second point referred to in the opening paragraph of this introduction. Clearly, whilst the approach adopted by many teachers involved 'experiential' learning and project work (as perhaps one would have anticipated), there were a number who had already seen the possibilities inherent in fiction for helping children to explore their thoughts and feelings in this area.

Approaching the topic through fiction has several advantages. It can provide an introduction to a particular difficulty or disability in a way that is less traumatic than a visit. It can act as a bridge between traditional and progressive approaches to curricula. It can deal with aspects which for one reason or another cannot easily be dealt with in any other way. I am thinking, for example, of the disruption to family life caused by the birth of a mentally disabled child or even more delicate matters like sexuality in adolescence for the physically disabled. Most importantly, however, fiction can provide a total picture of the experience of disability in the context of a story which captures the imagination of the reader. The child reads him or herself into the world created by the author, and by doing so begins to see, almost without realising it, how disability functions in a particular social, emotional and even historical context. Thus, the complexities and ambiguities of the topic can be dealt with in a way which the young reader is able to grasp. The author may choose, for example, to see the world through the young eyes of a child with special needs or a sibling or a friend of such a child, and in doing so manage to convey a sense of the complexity of their psychology — the confusions, contradictions, likes and dislikes, feelings about other people's attitudes, frustrations, hopes, fears, etc. Moreover, approaching the topic in this way means that its separateness as a topic is not overemphasised, and disability is dealt with in the context of lessons where the general aim is to explore all forms of human relationships.

It was with these thoughts in mind that I embarked on a project aimed at gathering together a number of children's novels where one or more of the central characters had a disability or difficulty. This was a fairly easy task because there is quite an abundance of such fiction, particularly by American publishers. My first impression on reading it was that most of the books were of a very poor quality from a number of points of view. I was not surprised by this. Because of the emotive nature of the topic, as well as the sentimentality which has traditionally surrounded the 'handicapped', there has clearly been a tendency for reviewers to be too kind to authors who include disabled characters in their stories. The reviews have tended, therefore, to lack critical bite. As Baskin and Harris (1977) point out, critical analysis of these books has often been by-passed because it is too often assumed that any book where a disabled person is a central character 'serves an important social goal'. Reviews typically consist of description of the story with little attempt at serious evaluation. Clichés abound — a 'heart-warming story' or 'one that serves as an inspiration to those similarly afflicted'.

What I have attempted to do in this book is to provide reviews which do not fall into this trap. However, there seemed little point in overemphasising the negative, and so for the most part I have chosen to discuss works which I believe to be of value. Of course, some 'bad' books have been included, for the sake of contrast, and other books which are mediocre or only good in parts have crept in because of the way the overview has been organised.

Inevitably, my personal perspective on the literature will emerge in the course of the discussion and there is no need to expand on it at length in this introduction. I clearly have an axe to grind, but hopefully it will be one with which the reader will sympathise! My first source of inspiration referred to above obviously influences the criteria employed in evaluating the fiction. To put it bluntly, my prime question about a book is to what extent is it compatible with and enhancing of integrationist ideals? This is sufficiently vague to leave the reader in some doubt as to what to expect! And this is deliberate because if this question could be answered in a few paragraphs then there would not have been much point in writing a whole book.

However, there is no doubt that I would like the reader to bear this question in mind right from the outset, even when skimming the pages before actually reading the book. In fact, I would like him or her to consider the possibility that the project I have embarked upon here is itself dubious. Maybe even to attempt to separate out a body of literature dealing with 'disability' is itself a discriminatory act and counterproductive in terms of furthering integrationist ideals? The literature on special education is strewn with failed attempts to write about children with special needs in a way which encourages their integration but which ultimately reinforces their marginalisation as a separate group. Even the Warnock Report (Dept. of Education and Science, 1978) can be criticised for treating children with special needs as if they constituted too much of a separate and clearly definable group, despite repeated denials by the Committee that this was what they were doing. As I have written elsewhere:

The new forms of categorisation recommended by Warnock are, of course, hedged with qualifications aimed at underplaying the possibility of these ever becoming as fixed and reified as the old forms. For many children assessed as having special needs it is hoped the status will be temporary because, since their learning difficulties are only mild or moderate and only a relatively small change is required in existing educational arrangements, a long period of special treatment is not envisaged. There will be a large number of children diagnosed as requiring some form of special help at some stage of their careers, but for many of these appropriate support in ordinary classes is all that will be needed. Also, it is obviously accepted by the authors that the prevalence can vary from one area to another and that factors in school, particularly secondary school 'reduce the occurrence of learning and behavioural difficulties' (see para. 18.15). This paragraph also refers to the 'updating of epidemiological studies such as the Isle of Wight Study in order to obtain information about changes in the prevalence of different handicapping conditions, including regional differences'. Nevertheless, none of these qualifications prevents the authors basing their policy recommendations on the assumption of a fixed percentage of children who are likely to be in need. (Quicke, 1981, p. 62)

This being so, it will only be a matter of time before the new descriptions of disabilities and difficulties advocated in the Report will become labels in the negative sense of the term.

When contemplating the organisation of this book, it would have been easy for me to have unwittingly contributed to furthering this re-labelling process. I could, for example, have listed a number of disabilities and difficulties — physical, visual, auditory, mental, educational — and grouped books according to which of these they dealt with. So that all books which had a blind hero or heroine would be discussed in one chapter, all those with a deaf character in another, and so on. What would have been wrong with this? The main fault, in my view, would have lain in the assumption that novels about human relationships and experiences in relation to one disability or difficulty were intrinsically different from those associated with another disability or difficulty. As if family conflict, for example, were different in kind for different disabilities. Now this is clearly not the case. Relationships may be similar across disabilities and profoundly different within the same disability. The mistake here is analogous to that made by advocates of segregated provision when they assumed that if children had the same disability they all had similar special educational needs. We now know that this was an erroneous view, and it was one of the reasons why Warnock advocated the abandonment of the old system of categorisation (para. 3.23).

I have attempted to avoid this pitfall by grouping books for discussion under common themes rather than under labels of disability or difficulty. The reader will have to judge whether this has been a successful approach or not. As it happens, certain chapters are about one disability or difficulty, but this is only because some of the themes have been dealt with more profoundly in relation to this particular form. For instance, the closeness of the relationship between a sibling and a disabled brother or sister can be explored in relation to any disability, since any disabled child may have such a relationship. But it seemed to me that the most insightful writing on this theme was to be found in novels where the close relationship was between a 'normal' and mentally disabled sibling, and therefore, the books in Chapter 2, 'The Special Relationship', are concerned with that rather than any other disability.

However, I would still like to advise the reader to be on guard against any tendency to assume that what is written and discussed is in some way peculiar to a particular group of children. Most of the problems around which the plots are constructed are those faced by many children disabled or not. Although some of the problems are disability specific, they are not necessarily the most profound or significant. It could be that ultimately the most difficult problems are to do, for example, with establishing identities, communicating with others in a divided society and overcoming feelings of inferiority, and that these are experienced, as such, in some form or another, by the majority of people in our society, not just a marginal group of disabled people.

A number of other points should be made about my approach. Although each chapter has a main theme, this does not mean that other themes are not discussed or that all the books concerned have only the one major theme. Some have a multiplicity of themes, but I have teased out the one which is salient for the chapter. In most cases I have included a fairly detailed description of the plot, or at least part of the plot so that the reader will understand what the book is about and what other themes are touched upon.

Another important point, which relates to the issue of the possible counter-productiveness of a project like this, is that it is obviously problematic as to what books might be included under the term 'disability' or even under 'difficulty' or 'special educational need'. The readers should ask themselves what they expect here. What picture is conjured up in their minds by the term disability, for example? Maybe they will immediately think of children in wheelchairs or children with hearing aids. But these constitute only a fraction of those who would be considered as having special educational needs in the broad Warnock sense of the term. What about children with mild or moderate learning difficulties or temporary emotional problems? Should books concerned with these difficulties be included? If so, then a case could probably be made out for choosing for discussion just about any modern children's novel! A slight exaggeration perhaps, but it makes the point that a line has to be drawn somewhere if the number of books is to be manageable.

I have raised this question because it relates to the issue referred to above concerning the organisation of material. Most of the books chosen are in fact about what might be described as obvious disabilities — physical, sensory, mental — and in selecting these I am fully aware of the possibility that the only consequence might be that the reader comes away with a concept of disability, difficulty or special need which is restricted to a small group of children, conveniently packaged as a discrete group and therefore perhaps more amenable to segregationist policies.

I can only hope that this will not happen. There are two reasons why I think that it will not. First, it is clear from what has been said already that it is the human relationships within which the disability is contextualised which are the main focus, not the disability itself.

The reader should understand this and draw the appropriate conclusions. Secondly, I have selected some (a minority of) books where the child character has a mild emotional disorder or a moderate or mild learning difficulty, partly to demonstrate that such children could be included although one would not use the term disability to describe their condition. The title of the book, however, is I think justified because the majority of texts do involve a child or adult with an obvious disability.

I must confess to one more qualm before allowing the reader to follow his or her own path! It is to do with the balance of coverage between disabilities. It is self-evident that the treatment of disability in much children's fiction will bear the marks of the culture of the society and the historical period in which it was written. Thus, in early children's fiction the disabled characters were treated in a more sentimental and romantic way than they are in the 'best' literature of today. Also, in earlier periods, the descriptions of disabilities were relatively undifferentiated. A child was 'blind' or 'lame' but degrees of sightedness or different forms of physical handicap were not part of the language available at the time. It is a characteristic of more recent fiction that authors are more up to date in this respect (although this can have disadvantages, a point I shall expand on later), and use terminology which reflects the interventions of professions like doctors or psychologists in the modern period. However, what has not changed a great deal is the dominance of certain disabilities like blindness and physical handicap in terms of their popularity as characteristics of disabled persons in novels — a popularity which has nothing to do with the severity of the disability or the numbers involved, but more to do with the public's perception of the nature of the 'handicap' and the manipulations of the public mind by charitable bodies. I have attempted to avoid reinforcing this dominance by deliberately selecting novels about less popular disabilities like mental disability or deafness, but there is still a tendency for the blind, for example, to figure more than they should from a statistical viewpoint (see Tringo, 1970).

Finally, I should like to draw the reader's attention to the two lists of references A and B, at the end of the book. List A consists of the novels discussed in the main body of the book, while list B contains all other references. Many of the references in the second list are to texts which have a social and psychological scientific bent, and this reflects my reliance on ideas and findings from that literature when discussing and evaluating novels. Since I am a social psychologist this is probably not surprising. One's response to novels inevitably reflects one's personal background, training and current intellectual and emotional concerns. However, from a more general viewpoint, I am aware there is a problematic here concerning the interaction between literature and social psychology (see Potter, Stringer and Wetherell, 1984) which is not explored in this text, and I acknowledge that the implicit 'truth and insight' view which informs most of the discussion would, in another sort of book, require more explanation and justification.

2 THE SPECIAL RELATIONSHIP

It is a popular view amongst the supporters of integration that there is no 'intrinsic' barrier to participation in community life for the majority of disabled people. By 'intrinsic' is meant inseparable from the nature of the disability itself, as if such a barrier was inevitably and always associated with that disability. Rather, they would argue that the barriers which do exist are due in the main to society's unwillingness to make the necessary alterations both at an institutional and attitudinal level that would accommodate people with disabilities and allow them to live fuller lives.

The plausibility of this view is evident if one considers the case of a physically handicapped person whose negotiation of the environment is facilitated by various simple alterations, such as the provision of ramps at the entrance to public buildings and doors which are wide enough for wheelchairs. Or the case of a person who has epileptic fits and whose life chances are improved by the removal of prejudice and fear about his or her condition.

However, some disabilities are so severe that they do present barriers to integration that appear to be insurmountable. I write 'appear' because I am working on the assumption that even in the most severe cases there is often more that can be done than many people imagine. Often the question is one of the humanity of the person and whether that humanity can be recognised by another person. If it can, then some form of integration and participation in community life is possible. Humanity and its recognition are, of course, difficult to define, but without entering into a deep philosophical discussion I propose that we can be said to recognise it if we can sense the potential in that person for achieving self-respect, for giving and receiving affection and for developing some understanding of the nature of community life — its rules and values (see Weinberg, 1981).

In a sense, persons with severe disabilities represent the acid test of our values, because it is this group which pose the most serious challenge to the rhetoric of integration. Relating to them does involve a struggle, but the history of special education is full of examples of successful, or at least partially successful outcomes. Some 'conditions' are no longer beyond the pale — like feeblemindedness, for example,

12

which has been reconstructed as a 'normal' variation of learning difficulty, or 'lunacy' which is now popularly interpreted as being as much to do with the situation as the person. The hope of educational approaches has replaced the pessimism of some old-fashioned medical ones.

The struggle has been nowhere more acute than in relation to severely mentally disabled children. From the foregoing it is plain that it is not enough that we should merely 'care' for children thus classified. Rather we should strive to appreciate their potential for living with us rather than apart from us and for having a dignified existence in their own right.

This may seem a very tall order. Who could adopt this progressive view if the child concerned was, say, a four-year-old girl, blind and mentally retarded, who spent most of her time and seemed to gain most pleasure from poking her fingers deep into the sockets of her eyes, often getting eye infections as a result? Or the child or adult who had become a 'vegetable' or a 'cot-and-chair' case, as some mentally handicapped people in subnormality hospitals are derogatorily described. And yet even in these extreme cases it is clear on closer examination that some attempt at rational behaviour or communication is often being made. Two people who express this are Newson and Hipgrave (1982), who suggest that we try to work out if the little girl's behaviour is worthwhile to her. It is perhaps, when you consider that

Debbie is in the dark and she doesn't have very creative ideas. She can't see what there is to play with and she bumps herself when she tries to explore. She'll need a lot of help to find anything more interesting than the flashes of light she 'sees' when she pokes at her eyes. She's also not aware that poking leads to infections, because the infection doesn't immediately result (pp. 15–16)

Likewise, Ryan and Thomas (1980) point out in relation to so-called 'vegetables' and 'cot-and-chair' cases 'anyone in close contact with such extremely handicapped people . . . in fact learns the barely perceptible ways in which they express their preferences, their reactions to events around them'.

There is no doubt that for these authors human life is there. Nevertheless, if we are to be honest, many will not be convinced by this. For them, a certain level of humanity will have been demonstrated but not sufficient to justify integration. A particularly powerful argument for segregation here is concerned with the effects such a child may have on family life and in particular on the happiness and progress of other children in the family. Such severely disabled children, it might be argued, should be 'put away' not so much for their own good but for the good of others.

However, the case here is by no means clear cut even for families with the most severely disabled and behaviourally problematic children. 'Normal' children do not necessarily gain from being sheltered from those dubbed 'abnormal', as if the latter were somehow contagious as well as disruptive. The research evidence is equivocal but clearly a great deal depends on the circumstances. Thus, Gath (1978) suggests that whether or not a sibling is adversely affected will depend on a variety of factors, e.g. social class of the family, family size, age of the 'normal' child at the birth of the disabled child; and Darling (1979) refers to the effect depending on the nature of the handicap, the degree of parental anxiety and the sex of the sibling – girls being more at risk than boys because they are more likely to be required to be involved in the care and management of their disabled brother or sister.

It is also possible, of course, that far from being adversely affected the development of the normal sibling is enhanced by the presence of a sibling who is clearly not going to follow the same path. The gains made in social maturity, sensitivity to the needs of disabled people than himself and a 'realistic' approach to problems may outweigh the disadvantages of having to baby-sit or having rather less of the parents' attention than ideal or the embarrassment which is sometimes felt when 'normal' friends come round. The only general statement that can be made is that reactions vary all the way from one extreme – as when the normal siblings anticipate taking on the burden of responsibility when the parents die – to the other when the sibling is disowned – 'don't tell anyone he's my brother'.

It is with these considerations in mind that I have chosen to discuss in this chapter a number of books where the narrative is set in the context of a family where there is a severely mentally disabled offspring, and in particular a family where one sibling is portrayed as being close to and having a special relationship with this offspring. Most of the books are written in the first person of this sibling, and one aim is to describe and analyse the changing reactions of the narrator to a series of traumatic events culminating in some form of crisis situation, which is eventually resolved or partly resolved, usually ambiguously. Few authors have attempted to portray the world through the eyes of disabled children themselves. This is understandable because in reality a severely disabled child can only be understood via the perceptions of the 'normal' sibling, which is why the relationship is so significant, so special. Each of the books will be evaluated primarily in relation to the optimism/pessimism theme referred to above — that is, in relation to the degree to which the reader is left with a belief in the humanity of the disabled child and the possibility of a successful outcome for the family, but particularly for the sibling with the special relationship. Each of the first four books to be discussed involve a character who is mentally disabled, or, in Warnock terminology, who has severe learning difficulties, and the last two a character who is also severely emotionally disturbed or, more accurately, non-communicating or 'autistic'.

A Girl With Her Own Kind of Sense

In Fanta Shyer's *Welcome Home, Jellybean* we are left in no doubt right from the start of the author's attitude towards residential institutions for the 'subnormal'. The book begins with the family of Geraldine, a thirteen-year-old mentally handicapped girl, venturing forth to the instititution to bring her home for good. Neil, her twelve-year-old brother and the narrator, describes the meal time he observed while they were waiting for Gerry.

All the kids were wearing the same big white bibs marked 'Green Valley Regional Training Centre' and they were all eating off plastic plates. They didn't have knives or forks though, just little spoons. And everybody was eating the same thing — no kidding — baby food. On every plate was a little orange pile of baby food and a little grey pile of what looked like the same stuff. There were older people here too, some who looked older than my father, and they were wearing bibs and eating baby food too. Some were being forced to eat it. Attendants were holding their jaws open and spooning it into their mouths. I saw my mother turn her head away and I didn't much want to look either, so we allowed ourselves to be ushered right out again the way we'd come, but not before I'd seen that a lot of the people there, seated at the long tables, were tied into their chairs with heavy leather straps. (pp. 10–11)

Those familiar with life in subnormality hospitals in Britain will not be surprised by this. It is no exaggeration, all the more horrific for being described in this simple, matter-of-fact way. We can understand immediately why this regime is so inhuman. There is no need for the author to go on to describe the even worse features of some of these institutions (like the sadism masquerading as caring, so graphically documented by Ryan and Thomas (1980)) in order for us to be persuaded that Gerry would stand a better chance at home, even if at this point in the book we do not know what home is like.

This is an important starting point. It rules out of court the institutional solution. Even the young Neil can see that life in such institutions lacks dignity, and he is as pleased as anyone that Gerry is coming home. If he had not observed the regime in the centre, and the necessity for his sister's removal, then the disruption to his own life would have seemed to him, as indeed it would have to the reader, an even greater and totally unjustified imposition. As it is, we are forced to weigh the horrors of the institution in the balance, when assessing the impact of Geraldine on Neil's development and on the family generally. And this impact has many negative features. Neil's own life is affected in a number of ways. She interferes with his homework, keeps him awake at night and presents one enormous control problem for the whole household. Eventually, Neil starts handing in school assignments late and gets into trouble with the teachers, who do not initially seem to understand what is wrong with him. He observes changes in his mother which upset him — 'My mother was getting those circles under the eyes that old people get and she was hardly smiling anymore'. Father is critical of the way mother handles Geraldine, but does not seem to want to help her constructively and opts out by leaving home and moving into a flat of his own, whence he maintains a relationship with Neil, even suggesting that if Neil could not 'take it any more' he should move in with him. Yet, for all this, there is a positive side which Fanta Shyer manages to convey without lapsing into romanticism or sentimentality. All the small but significant improvements in Geraldine are in keeping with what we can realistically expect of a child with this degree of mental handicap. Neil is not so overwhelmed by the burden of physical caring that he cannot, at times, take on the role of Gerry's teacher and gradually acquire insights into her mental functioning. He observes for example, that her actions may not be done for what to adults are the 'right reasons' but there is reasoning there even though it is not always appreciated as such.

'It wasn't that Gerry didn't have any sense it was just that she had her own kind of sense, but Dad didn't understand that' (p. 112). He sees her taking gigantic steps forward in her own terms and realises that perhaps other people cannot see this. Even if her learning does result in 'virtuous errors', it is still learning. On one occasion she throws a bag of groceries down the rubbish chute because the last similar bag she saw was full of rubbish, and she thus demonstrates that she has learnt where to put rubbish. We see Neil teaching Geraldine, taking a great delight in her progress and learning something about himself as a result.

Even the fact of the parents breaking up is not a totally negative occurrence in terms of benefits to Neil. For the adult reader father's actions represent an opting-out, and although we can see life from his viewpoint, the worst of him has been brought out by the situation and his capacity for caring is clearly limited. A child may not understand this in the same way, but it is an indication of Neil's rapidly developing social and emotional awareness that we see him begin to look more objectively at father and eventually to see through him.

Dad rolled down the window to say goodbye when I'd gotten out of the car and all of a sudden I thought of what he'd said about his moustache, how it was uncomfortable and got on his nerves, so he'd decided to get rid of it – ffft – and no kidding, it was like being hit with an icy wind when I realized that the way he felt about his moustache was exactly the way he felt about us. (p. 112)

Nevertheless, whether or not Neil ultimately benefits is not presented as a cut-and-dried issue. It is difficult to predict the outcome, and we are kept in suspense on this point as the story unfolds. Neil's feelings are complex and colour his thinking – 'I understood, but I didn't really want to understand', and the question posed by father is the crucial one – just how much can he take? His life is disrupted, of that there is no doubt, and the final straw, maybe, is when Geraldine shouts out in the school concert and ruins his piano solo. But, in the final showdown, the joy he feels at the realisation that she can be taught things, his appreciation of her humanity, is enough to compensate for the bad times. And thus the final note of optimism: 'My sister, now smart enough to push the right elevator buttons, to say my name so anybody could understand it, to bring left overs to a dog – and getting smarter by the minute (p. 128).

It is to the author's credit that she manages to portray all this in a way which is tough and frank but at the same time full of fun and humour. Neil's character and development are the main preoccupation, but sketches of other characters, particularly the parents', though thinly drawn because from a child's viewpoint, are not stereotypally the overburdened mother and opting-out father. They come through as individuals reacting to adverse circumstances in a way with which we can sympathise. It is a pity, however, that the author did not extend her sensitivities to the portrayal of the hostile elements in the environment who are again, as in so many stories, represented by the rough, working-class bully. Neil divides the children at his school into four types

> There's the Jock bunch and they all hang out near the gym, and then there's the East End bunch, who all live in the same housing development and cluster upstairs in the corridor and there are the brains and they flock together near the maths office. There's also the music and drama set and they all clump together near the auditorium. (p. 19)

Neil feels that he does not fit in anywhere, but it is the East End bunch who produce the main villain of the piece, the deceitful and deviant Beefy. Unlike the music and drama set who could be pretty thoughtless but otherwise were 'regular guys', Beefy and his cronies could really hit you below the belt. 'What are you retarded or something? Does it run in your family?' says Beefy to Neil. There is an inconsistency here. On the one hand the author is keen to puncture the stereotype of mental handicap, but does so in a way that reinforces an equally pernicious stereotype based on class discrimination. I shall come back to this point in Chapter 4, but for now suffice it that it is a criticism to note when teaching the book (see Chapter 10).

I Love You, I Hate You

Neil gets annoyed and frustrated with Geraldine, but the book does not involve an exploration of some of the more powerful emotions of hate, jealousy, revulsion and guilt which can infuse the relationship between a disabled and non-disabled sibling. Neil can see the funny side, and is not the sort of person who allows himself to be eaten away by self-hate. Unlike Dorrie in Rodowsky's *What About Me?* we do not feel he is at risk of becoming embittered or in some way scarred emotionally. However, it is part of the diverse pattern of family life that profound negative feelings are often experienced by one sibling about another and this is a relatively normal feature which in the case of a family with a disabled offspring can take on greater proportions. This is the situation for the heroine of Rodowsky's moving and compassionate novel.

For Dorrie at the beginning of the story, hate for her eleven-year-old Down's syndrome brother Fredlet is the emotion which is all but overpowering her and with which she is struggling to come to terms. It does not exist all the time, but when she does experience it it scares her. The problem is that she feels her own needs, indeed her own existence, are being ignored — What about me? — and that in her family Fredlet's needs seem to have first priority. Even the simple matter of mother asking her to baby-sit causes her pain, and understandably so from her viewpoint because mother does not even acknowledge that for Dorrie there is a sacrifice involved. It is just assumed that she will cancel all her own plans to look after him. Fredlet seems to mess up her life at certain crucial points, as when he embarrasses her at the school concert when he gets up and mimics the conductor, or when he smashes the ceramic cat she has won prize ribbons for. He embarrasses her on buses, and conversations with her mother on important matters are impossible when he's around. She can see nothing positive in him, no signs of improvement, and life is at best boring and repetitious, and at worst she even finds herself in a situation where she regards him as physically repulsive. She cannot stand the ways adults patronise him, patting him on the head and telling him not to worry, and she is aware that her mother's own career in art has been replaced by making a career of Fredlet. Nevertheless, (although clearly when the novel begins it is a hate period) her emotions are mixed. 'I can absolutely loathe him one minute, and then he'll do something — maybe just like laugh — and then I have to love him — for a while anyway' (p. 10).

Although the author's picture of Dorrie's relationship with her parents is typical of many that can be found in children's novels, there is an interesting build up to the reader's 'discovery' of the true nature of these relationships. We start by seeing life through Dorrie's eyes, but gradually become aware that her mother and father are not the monsters they seem to her on occasion. They have a viewpoint which is not always clear to her, but has its own validity even if this is not always spelt out for the reader. They themselves are struggling to cope with a difficult situation, a point which the reader can see more easily than Dorrie. In the end, having taken the decision to move away from New York so that they can be nearer the family and live in a house with better facilities, they are aware enough of Dorrie's needs to understand that she would like to stay in the big city at least until she finishes high school, and are prepared to go along with the plan for her to stay with Guntzie, Dorrie's art teacher, guru, neighbour and friend of the family.

Much of the tension within Dorrie is generated by her failure to communicate with her father and mother, and by their failure in much of the story, to appreciate her perspective, although we feel they perhaps understand more than Dorrie thinks. She is exasperated by various failed attempts at conversation with either parent, so much so that on one occasion it is too much for her and she takes flight.

One of the more profound insights of the book concerns the way the heroine's perception of Fredlet changes when she sees him away from the emotionally charged home environment. In contrast to Neil in *Welcome Home, Jellybean*, Dorrie's closeness to Fredlet does not result in her being an accurate observer of his development, because her perception of him is too distorted by negative emotions and so egocentric that the realisation Fredlet has a life outside the family comes as a surprise to her. When she sees him in the school setting where she has asked to be placed for her work-study (a positive move on her part) and realises that many of her reactions are specific to Fredlet rather than mentally disabled children generally, we see her beginning to come to terms with her jealousy and fears. She has to admit to herself that some other people like him quite a lot, that he has a personality for them and that it gave her 'a strange feeling to see Fredlet having a life other than the one at home' (p. 67).

The main emotional learning in the book, however, comes from her conversations with Guntzie, a person she admires and whose advice is important to her. It is by way of these conversations that the author cleverly explores taboo areas about which little has been written in the research literature, like the admission on the part of a child that they feel repulsed by their mentally disabled sibling.

Guntzie stings her with home truths which pull her up short and force her to reflect on her feelings. She, Dorrie, has called her brother an animal, not because she did not mean to, but because at the time of saying it she really did feel it, really did find him repulsive, a genuine feeling which her father refused to acknowledge and therefore was unable to understand her emotional turmoil. Guntzie, however, accepts her negative feelings, and tries to show her that she must accept them before she can consider more positive ways of dealing with them. The interchange takes place in Guntzie's flat to which Dorrie has taken flight:

'Oh, today was beautiful. I went to help my mother take Fredlet to the dentist and I ran out and left them there. I got up out of that waiting room and left. Just left.'

'Why?'

Guntzie's word sounded like a shot. She got up and went over to the cabinet under the window and came back with a stack of prints and started sorting them. But still, that 'Why' was waiting for me. 'Why? I don't know why. Yes I do. Because he was howling like an animal and I didn't know what to do. And I'm, I'm – oh, I don't know.'

I squashed the lump of clay as hard as I could and began rolling it into a coil.

'Have you selected a print for your acrylic painting yet?'

I look at Guntzie as if I really hadn't heard her.

'Have I done what?'

'Have you gotten your canvas ready yet?'

Guntzie jumped up and put the prints into the file cabinet, then gathered up the mugs.

'What's that got to do with anything?' I asked, struggling up out of the beanbag chair.

'It has everything to do with it, Dorrie.' Guntzie put the cups in the sink and went to sit in front of the easel with carrousel on it.

'Fredlet's not going to get much smarter.' Guntzie was one of the few people who ever talked right out about how smart Fredlet was, or rather, how smart Fredlet wasn't. 'And plenty of times you're going to think he's repulsive.'

'But he is repulsive. Sometimes I can't stand him or Mum or Dad either.'

'Or yourself?'

'Yes, or me either. And I can't wait till college or after to be really free.'

'Sometimes freedom isn't all that free. Anyway what have you done that's constructive?'

'I was beginning to wish I'd stayed at the dentist's . . . ' (pp. 44-5)

Guntzie then picks up a casual remark of Dorrie's about Fredlet's reaction to her ceramic cat and demonstrates how there might be more to Fredlet than Dorrie realises.

'Poor Cat. That's what Fredlet calls it'.

'I know. I've heard him. He must see something in it.'

'What could he see?' I asked, still feeling the sting of Guntzie's words.
'I don't know. We'll never know, but he sees something. Something only for Fredlet. The way we were talking at the museum about the Kandinsky. Something for everyone who wants to look. Even Fredlet . . .' (p. 46)

Dorries comes to recognise that at least part of the problem is within herself and it is her coming to terms with this that constitutes the main developmental line of the book. In fact, she cracks down hard on herself, calling herself a monster on occasions and surrendering to feelings of guilt particularly at one point when she feels responsible for having made her mother cry — 'Could I have done that? And suddenly I was very frightened to think that possibly something I had done could hurt her that much.' (p. 83).

This novel is worth reading for the way it deals with the powerful emotions which are generated in families by the presence of a severely disabled offspring, and the ambiguous feelings of an adolescent girl as she moves towards maturity to become more objective in her judgement of people and events and adjusted to the constraints of her environment. However, unlike Neil, Dorrie's effort to adjust is simply one of coming to terms with reality and she does not play much part in creating that reality. She sees Fredlet in a different light once the distortion due to faulty perception is removed, but we do not find the joy here that Neil feels when he witnesses the successful outcome of a teaching intervention which he made off his own bat, so to speak, as part of his personal way of helping, improving and changing his sister. The adaptation model of adolescence which underpins *What About Me?* is critically evaluated in Chapter 7.

Another misgiving I have about the book is the way it ends. Fredlet dies just before the family uproots itself from New York, and we are left wondering if the author intends us to feel that this is probably the best outcome. To put it bluntly Fredlet, having served his purpose in helping Dorrie to mature, promptly leaves the stage. Is this a happy ending? For Dorrie it is; she still feels that she has a brother —

'I was glad that Fred had been my brother. Had been and still was, and always would be. Always would be in the way that everyone we've known is part of us. All tangled up in our lives. The way we're tangled up in theirs.' (p. 134)

Maybe so, but would she have liked to have been 'tangled up' with a live Fredlet for the rest of her life? The reader suspects not, but since he is dead our thinking stops there. There is nothing for the reader or the characters to anticipate: for example, as to whether Dorrie was now so fully in control of her own emotions that a wild swing of mood (perhaps in the direction of hatred again?) would have been unlikely. The only question we are left with is: Is it better for her that he is dead? If so, what value can be placed on his life? This is not the sort of question that should be raised at the end of a book which one wants to value for not querying whether life is better than no life at all, but for showing that one form of life is no less worthy of the name than another.

Why Can't Molly Be?

A similar ambiguity in relation to the death of the disabled character occurs at the climax of Paton Walsh's *Unleaving*, but whereas in Rodowsky's book the ambiguity is unnecessary and anomalous, in this book the question of the best outcome – life or death? – is pivotal. The values underpinning this book are far less progressive than those guiding the authors of *Welcome Home, Jellybean* and *What About Me?*, and it is doubtful if the older and more academically inclined adolescents for whom this book is intended will come away from it with a more sympathetic attitude to mental disablement. The book is worth discussing partly because the author is well known (her other books include *Fireweed* and *Goldengrove*) and partly because the book is well written, and contains some evocative description, interesting dialogue and subtle interplay between characters. Yet for all this, one feels that if the author's aim was to throw light on the nature of life in intellectualising academic families or even introduce philosophical ideas into a children's novel there were many ways that this could have been achieved without reference to mental handicap, and without having to create a crude, inconsistent and negative portrait of a Down's syndrome child.

The story is set in beautiful sea and coastal scenery in Cornwall. Madge has inherited Goldengrove, the large, family house, and on the suggestion of her headmistress has invited a university reading party to use it for the summer. The party is led by Professor Tregeagle who has two children – the moody Patrick and 'mongoloid' Molly. Patrick intrigues Madge because he is clearly a complex and rather sad person who has 'weather in his face, endless changes. Like the sea below, he changes abruptly, varying wildly from one mood to another, and at worst ferocious, frightening.' (p. 67).

Molly is described as having a 'face which is very ruddy, with almond-shaped pale blue eyes and hardly any lashes'. At first she repulses Madge, who seeing the smile which 'fills with spittle and oozes down the chin' is sickened for an instant, but she fights against and overcomes her feelings of revulsion. Madge is clearly sympathetic, but we never observe her getting close to Molly or behaving towards her in a way that brings the best out in Molly. For example, she allows herself to become 'stupefied with boredom' when playing with her, because she cannot persuade her to play any game other than picking up shells and handing them to Madge and taking them back again. This does not surprise us because although these are more than token gestures for Madge and represent a genuinely sympathetic response to the 'weak in mind', they are not based on any knowledge of Molly's characteristics, or even the intuitive understanding of the special sibling. In this case, though, the special sibling Patrick is too much of a tortured soul to apply his special knowledge to good effect. In one bizarre scene, for example, we see him trying to teach Molly to say 'cogito ergo sum'. Madge is disgusted because she recognises the cruel and desperate meaning of this act. Earlier, Professor Tregeagle had made his insensitive contribution for all to hear in the presence of Molly.

'Which is', said Professor Tregeagle 'that no idea alleged to be innate, even the simplest, does in fact command universal assent.' Behind him the bobbing golden heads of the children dip and bounce between the sunlit stones. 'For it is evident that children and idiots have not the least apprehension or thought of them.'

Madge stared at Molly, whose coarse features and sluggish understanding are thus enough to strip the soul of God's fingerprints . . . (p. 56)

This is typical of the Professor — an academic who splits the intellectual from the emotional side of life, a rather stereotypal characterisation but one which serves to make an important point in this context, because it is this feature of family life which has resulted in Patrick's emotional instability and aloneness.

'We're not allowed feelings in my family', said Patrick. 'Only thoughts. So if one has feelings, one has them alone. That's partly why my father can't do with Molly. She has feelings all right – simple ones. But she'll never have anything he would call a thought.' (p. 84)

In trying to teach Molly to say 'cogito' Patrick is trying magically to make her seem human in her father's eyes. Madge later confronts Tregeagle with these stark facts of his perception of Molly, and expresses her distaste for his abstract style of philosophical debate which excludes emotion and leads to the dehumanisation of his daughter.

Towards the end of the book Molly is killed when she falls off the top of a cliff. Both Madge and her brother Paul see the incident, see Patrick stick out his hand before she goes over, and place their own interpretations on this action. Patrick himself does not really know whether or not he intended to push her over, but he is certain that he has often felt like killing her, and this is enough for him to be wracked with guilt over the incident. Yet, in describing his arguments with himself, he eventually reveals what he had been thinking all along, that perhaps it may have been for the best.

'I expected to feel dreadful. I expected to feel crushed by guilt . . . I knew I would. And I thought that was nothing, nothing compared to what she would suffer as she grew to know dimly what other people felt about her. She wasn't as bad as they thought, Madge, she was going to partly know . . . she had a mother who just despaired about her, and a father who thinks the intellect is immortal and souls resemble bodies . . . and me.' (p. 131)

Madge is asked by Patrick to judge his actions. She opts out by saying that that is not the way she thinks, and yet we feel she has forgiven him and is reserving all her anger for his father, whom she sees as the basic cause of the inhumanity.

However, although Madge recognises the faulty attitudes which have produced Patrick's confusion and instability, such that his special relationship with Molly is in a sense, warped, she does not see what we as a critical audience would like her to see, that there are positive ways of looking at and dealing with children like Molly. The author seems so concerned to portray the moral dilemmas through Patrick, faced as he is with what at one time seemed to him an unending struggle against an intractable environment, that she is compelled to treat Molly as a fixed point at one extremity of humanity, part of the unchanging burden. Having this function for the plot it is inevitable that Molly is always seen in a negative, stereotypal way. There is virtually nothing encouraging said about Molly by any of the characters — not about her looks, or emotions or desire for social contact, and even Madge is 'stupefied with boredom' when she plays with her.

And yet according to Patrick 'she wasn't as bad as they thought . . . she was going to partly know.' This knowledge of Molly's nature from the mouth of the sibling with the special relationship, the one with the closest contact and therefore an authoritative view, plus other observations on her activity and demeanour scattered throughout the book, suggests that there might be a lot more to Molly then even Madge recognises. Is she not a Down's syndrome child who would be considered to be high-grade? If so, and it seems to be so, then we could expect her to be capable of leading a fairly independent life when she was older. Both father and son ask the question — What of the future? There is no reply from any other character and the question is clearly intended to be rhetorical. But we know there can be quite a rosy future for such children. It is a mistake, for example, to think that all children with Down's syndrome are very similar just because they all share the same chromosome defect (see Booth, 1982, p. 28). We know they are not all severely mentally disabled, there is great variability in their development, and the average life expectancy is about 40 years. Many people who work with such children know that they can be loving, humourous and independent, and can participate in and contribute to the life of the community.

But these features are not considered in the moral equation presented here, even for Madge, and we are left wondering if this is just because the author is ignorant about Down's syndrome or whether such aspects are not emphasised because for the characters in the story they would have been dismissed as relatively inconsequential in any case. Whatever the child's potential, the types of interpersonal relationships idealised and valued in the book are light years away from anything one might expect of a relationship between a high-grade Down's syndrome and a 'normal' person. It is a perfect irony of the book that whilst the central character Madge attacks Professor Tregeagle for his intellectual elitism, she herself thinks of relationships in terms of what might be dubbed emotional elitism of the navel contemplating, self-indulgent variety, perhaps peculiar to people in certain literary circles. One of her conversations with Patrick exemplifies this. The two of them are talking about the differences between themselves and adults, and how they find it almost impossible to conceive of themselves as becoming adult and caring about the things adults care about. Patrick suggests 'I think, you know, they have secret consolation . . . The lucky ones have love for someone. And it makes a private world nobody else can see at all. Then they're all right.' (p. 92).

They go on to discuss the notion of love which, Madge suggests if it is to involve real happiness, must mean 'having one's favourite self, the person one most likes to be, loved by someone.' To which Patrick replies:

'And that's not all either. Because I don't think it's one's favourite self exactly — I mean not necessarily the person one flatters oneself one is, like I fancy myself as a great pianist — I think it's the nearest self — the one one truly is. And I don't think being loved by just anyone will do it either; I think it has to be a special person . . . I expect it doesn't happen very often. After all, people don't seem all that happy, by and large, do they?' (p. 93)

It is easy to see that if people are so pernickety about who they can and who they cannot 'truly love' then children like Molly will seem so beyond the pale that love may not even be an appropriate term to use when describing an affectionate relationship with them! Such a relationship is any case considered to have an unhealthy element. There is a suggestion of this in Patrick's description of his mother's relationship with Molly when she is referred to as being 'all ground down under caring'. At root of Patrick's and Madge's interchange is a view of love so idiosyncratic and rarified as to exclude most human relationships from its embrace.

Unlike *Welcome Home, Jellybean* or *What About Me?*, which at least make some attempt to portray the mentally handicapped character as a person with various attributes, *Unleaving* leaves one with the impression that the child in question has very little character at all. Molly is used too much as a vehicle for raising questions about other characters, rather than as an individual in her own right. She is also a 'for instance' illustrating a point in a high-level argument. Madge is aware of this; but the author, unintentionally I suspect, makes her fall into a similar trap and the overall effect is to exclude Molly's character from the reader's sight.

I Know How He Feels

All these books can be contrasted with Byars's *The Summer of the*

Swans, which is altogether a much gentler and less complex story, suitable for age groups younger than those for whom the previous books are intended. The treatment of the special relationship is cosier because although we see Sarah being irritated by her disabled brother Charlie we are never in any doubt as to the affection she feels for him. Unlike Dorrie in *What About Me?* there are no see-saw feelings of love and hate, although Sarah certainly has her own problems, succinctly described early on in the book:

> Up until this year, it seemed, her life had flowed along with rhythmic evenness. The first fourteen years of her life all seemed the same. She had loved her sister without envy, her aunt without finding her coarse, her brother without pity. Now all that was changed. She was filled with a discontent, an anger about herself, her life, her family, that made her think she would never be content again.

In fact she is just as irritated by her sister Wanda as she is by Charlie. For instance, she objects to Wanda making Charlie the topic of conversation with her classmates — 'What do you say?' 'Let me tell you all about my retarded brother — it's so interesting.' Sarah is clearly sensitive on the topic of Charlie. She vigorously defends him if she feels he is being looked down upon or being exploited. She is so convinced a boy called Joe stole Charlie's watch that she 'hated him so much the sight of him made her sick', even though she did not really know if he was the thief.

Like many fathers with 'handicapped' offspring, Sarah's father seems to have opted out and become remote from the family. This is clearly a problem for her but not a pressing one. Her mother has been dead for six years, and father doesn't come home until the weekend, and even then he is not very communicative. Charlie became retarded after a series of illnesses when he was three and now 'can be lost and afraid three blocks from home and cannot speak one word to ask for help'. Sarah takes him to see the swans, and that night he thinks he sees a swan in the bushes outside his bedroom window, and tries to pursue it back to the lake. He gets lost. Next day the alarm is raised, and everyone starts looking for Charlie, including Joe, who teams up with Sarah for the search. They eventually find him and take him home.

The characters of Sarah and Charlie are well observed. This is one of the few books where whole chapters are devoted directly to the viewpoint of the disabled child. The author describes Charlie's feelings and reactions when alone and afraid. Another strength of the book is the way the author demonstrates through Sarah how the special relationship is experienced, and provides an insight into how such a relationship is built up. Sarah is telling Mary her friend how she can be sure which direction he took.

'I just know. There's something about me that makes me understand Charlie. It's like I know how he feels about things. Like sometimes I'll be walking down the street and I'll pass the jeweller's and I'll think that if Charlie were here he would want to stand right there and look at those watches all afternoon and I know right where he'd stand and how he'd put his hands up on the glass and how his face would look. And yesterday I knew he was going to love the swans so much that he wasn't ever going to want to leave. I know how he feels.'

'You just think you know.'

'No, I know. I was thinking about the sky one night and I was looking up at the stars and I was thinking about how the sky goes on and on forever, and I couldn't understand it no matter how long I thought, and finally I got kind of nauseated and right then I started thinking. Well, this is how Charlie feels about some things. You know how it makes him sick sometimes to try to print letters for a long time and . . .' (p. 91)

The Non-communicating Child

This insight into the inner life of the mentally disabled child is difficult to achieve without the intimate contact such as that which often develops between a child and a special sibling, but even this might be insufficient when the child is autistic. However close the relationship, there is always an apparently immovable block to communication, which is the reason for the more up-to-date label of non-communicating that is often attached to such a child. Some authorities doubt the wisdom of using a term like autism, but I shall use it in this instance because by definition there is less possibility of social contact ever being established with a mentally disabled child with autistic features, and from the standpoint of a concern that such a child's humanity should be recognised this autistic quality constitutes the greatest of all stumbling blocks.

Although non-communicating children are a fairly diverse group they have in common an apparently unsocial nature, and even for those who improve during adolescence social relationships and language problems are usually still evident. Often they appear to have more intelligence than their social behaviour would suggest, but this impression, often derived from observing some isolated ability they seem to have, e.g. a sensitivity to music, serves only to raise false hopes, and when these hopes are dashed parents and siblings feel even more pessimistic (see Furneaux, 1981).

The question posed in novels where the disabled character is autistic is similar to one already discussed in this chapter in relation to other books but written even larger: Can there or can there not be communication with these children?

Two books which portray families' reactions to the presence of a non-communicating child are Brown's *The Siblings* (retitled *Find Debbie*) and Spence's *The October Child*. These books have been chosen because they seem to me to provide an interesting contrast in the way the topic is handled. They differ in emotional tone, in the way they portray the moral dilemmas, and in the attitude adopted towards the question of integration, but above all in their treatment of the sibling relationships.

The Dutiful Son

The October Child is about what happens to the Mariner family after the arrival of Carl. The family are happy and close knit, and live in the small Australian coastal resort of Chapel Rocks. The problems created by Carl are discussed in detail. He dislikes any form of change, shrieks when he should be sleeping, is difficult to feed and relates to people as if they were objects. The story is concerned with the reactions of all the members of the family – Beth the mother, Robert the father, siblings Kenneth and Adrienne – but the main focus is on Douglas, the middle one of the three and the one who grows up to be the closest to Carl and who provides the most help to the parents in looking after him. The family move to Sidney so that Carl can go to school. This in fact suits Douglas because it means he can go to music school. Kenneth is more put out by the move and eventually, at 16, leaves home to join a band of religious hippies. Father is uneducated and not qualified enough for many jobs, but he manages to obtain a job in a bookshop and, though not well off, the family holds together.

Unlike some of the books already discussed in this chapter, there is some doubt as to whether the special relationship between Carl and Douglas has been mutually beneficial. Clearly, Carl has benefitted, but the reader is left wondering about Douglas. On the one hand, the latter has, perhaps, gained in social maturity, but on the other without the burden of Carl, what might he have achieved? It is this ambivalence which produces complex feelings within Douglas, which he is partially aware of himself. He has to come to terms with caring for and feeling a sense of responsibility towards Carl, whilst at the same time feeling concerned about the effect the 'burden' of Carl has on his mother, himself and the rest of the family.

There is nothing mysterious about Douglas's relationship with Carl. The author's description of how the specialness of the relationship came about is well observed. Douglas is a sensitive boy who has a talent for music. It is his singing to which the crying Carl responds. As he sings 'the whimpers came at longer and longer intervals' and Carl's crying gradually ceases. This is of great help to a weary mother, and thus Douglas is thrust permanently into the role of mother's aide, a role which, up to a point, he is glad to embrace because he is fed up with seeing his mother 'always busy and tired', often with an 'expression of utter misery and exhaustion on her face'. He feels that his prime duty is towards Carl and his mother, and his own personal wants take second place. In fact, he feels this so strongly that when he dreams of going away to music school it seems to him that by even contemplating such a venture he is letting his mother down. Like many young children, he feels his inner thoughts and feelings are an open book to his mother. Spence captures this beautifully. Douglas is dreaming of going to music school when: 'The appearance of his mother and Carl brought him back to earth and a sensation of guilt. He felt sure that some evidence of his disloyalty must have shown on his face but Beth hardly glanced at him.' (p. 61).

However, he does eventually get a chance to pursue his musical studies, and his own involvement with Carl does not result in a permanent block to his career development.

Unlike Douglas, older brother Kenneth does not have any special affinity to his non-communicating sibling. This is no stereotypal portrait of an opting-out or rejecting older sibling. He grows away from the family situation, but the author makes us feel this has a reasonableness about it which given the circumstances we can fully appreciate. As the author observes — 'Kenneth was the active one, the participant in events outside the home, the confident handler of his own problems.' We see him going through various adolescent stages, searching for an identity outside the home. He takes flight, but who can blame him? He is just not cut out to do a Douglas. His view of Douglas's predicament is predictable — 'The only thing for you to do is grow up fast and get out of here, otherwise you'll be stuck with Carl for the rest of your life.' (p. 127). This is not to suggest that he rejects Carl, although, like Douglas, he dislikes his mother's constant fussing over him. He merely wants to give his brother sound advice about the future. Perhaps, like Douglas, Kenneth does have dark thoughts about Carl which surface occasionally, but this is always in the context of his own struggles with identity crises and therefore *en passant* with no lasting bitterness.

Likewise, the author's treatment of the parents is sensitive and sympathetic. The mother, Beth, is portrayed as burdened, but not oppressed in a pathological sense. We feel her reactions are 'normal' reactions to oppressive circumstances. Crises in the family are brought about by an overburdened mother's thoughtlessness rather than by anything more psychologically unhealthy. The author provides some remarkable insights into just how such 'thoughtlessness' is experienced by a child. Douglas is making a bold attempt to live his own life and yet help the family cope with Carl. He loves music and has his own room where he keeps his precious record player and his own musical compositions. The door is always locked, but one day his mother accidentally leaves the door open when she has been cleaning the room. Carl gets in and as a result the arm of the record player is broken and Douglas's musical compositions defaced. Douglas cannot understand why Beth did not take more care, knowing how important that room was to him. On the one hand, she annoys him by a 'nagging insistence on neatness and orderliness and similar trivialities' and by concentrating her maternal energies more on him than any of her other children, and yet she forgets to lock his room. Perhaps it was just an accident, a moment of carelessness and that was all, but could it have been the first sign that mother was beginning to lose her grip? Douglas's overprotectiveness towards her seems to spring from such uncertainties. His mother loves him, but can she maintain it through thick and thin, with Carl wearing her down from day to day?

Unlike the stereotypal opting-out father, Douglas's father, Robert (we actually learn his Christian name, which is unusual!) has a great sense of responsibility and stays with the family. Like mother, he could also be thoughtless as far as Douglas was concerned, but basically was a caring father. However, we feel he is a victim of circumstances which go beyond the fact of having a non-communicating child. He has not been successful in life, but has managed to get by. The arrival of Carl is undoubtedly a blow. The struggle to survive eventually takes its toll of him. 'For the first time, Douglas saw him, not merely as a father, but as a tired, stooped and perpetually worried middle-aged man.' (p. 83).

A Horror Story

The Siblings (or *Find Debbie*) is basically a detective story, a gripping thriller, about a missing 'psychotic' fourteen-year-old girl. There is a misuse of terminology here because it is very unusual for a girl with these behavioural characteristics to be described as 'psychotic'. Inspector Bates and his sergeant are sent to find her, and they try to build up a picture of Debbie mainly from interviews with her brothers and sisters. He speaks to Ian her twin brother, her older brother Terry, a teacher married with one child, and her older sister Brenda, a librarian.

The shock-horror tone of the book generally is typified by Brown's description of Debbie as making a sound with 'the saliva in her throat . . . like a death rattle'. She is also described as 'exceptionally pretty', which is clearly used as a device for making us even more shocked by her monstrous behaviour. The author seems to be trading on the myth that beauty goes with 'goodness' and ugliness with 'badness' and therefore we would not normally expect such an 'exceptionally pretty' child to behave so badly.

The special relationship between Ian and Debbie is of a rather different order to that between Carl and Douglas. Here we are left in no doubt as to the negative effects on Ian, twin brother of Debbie. Unlike *The October Child* the family processes underpinning the development of the relationship are not described, and instead Brown uses the cliché of an uncanny understanding between twins to explain why Ian seems to have a way of getting through to Debbie and controlling her. 'They don't lock the doors when Ian is with Debbie'.

Like Douglas, Ian also has a musical talent. He plays Mozart sonatas on the violin, and Debbie, although she wrecks just about everything else in sight, never touches his violin, even when it is placed directly in front of her. But although this seems to involve a human response in Debbie's part, the author conveys to us that this is not so much an emergent trace of affection but rather a reflection of Ian's strange dominance over her. We are told elsewhere that the only time Debbie recognised the existence of her older brother Terry was when he hit her. The implication is that she does respond but unthinkingly and reflex like, as an animal cowering before the sheer physical power confronting it. And so the relationship neither brings out Debbie's humanity nor Ian's, whose development is distorted by his pathological association with her. Debbie is eventually found in the shallow grave at the house of a homicidal maniac called McKinley where Ian had taken her. Bates, the inspector, confronts Ian with his suspicions:

'But no illusions for you Ian – no sedatives. Only the stark reality of Debbie like a darkness of the soul. Debbie is your creation, you are her god – in you she lives and moves and has her being. Be careful, though Ian. It's making you arrogant. You'll end up thinking you have the power of life and death over her.' (p. 144)

Ian himself has become socially isolated. He has no friends because of what his relationship with Debbie has done to him.

Although the authors of *The Siblings* and *The October Child* both attempt to present us with stark reality, Spence does so in a way which allows us to make up our own minds about the healthiness or otherwise of the special relationship. In *The October Child* she displays the evidence, fragment by fragment, of the changing relationships in a way that makes her characterisations of people and events most convincing. The reader is allowed to observe with her. Brown, however, attempts to entice the reader into seeing a sinister and morbid set of relationships by importing non-proven assumptions about 'unnatural' communication between twins. If we refuse to take these on board, then there is nothing else on which to build a picture of the relationships. We are left hanging on Brown's cliché's, open mouthed at the horror of it all.

Similar points can be made about the representations of the attitudes and involvement of the other siblings. Like Kenneth in *The October Child*, Terry and Brenda in *The Siblings* both eventually escape from home leaving a younger sibling with the responsibility of helping mother to 'shoulder the burden'. They are both negative in their assessments of the possibilities for improvement in the disabling condition and in their estimation of the effects on the close sibling. However, the books have very little else in common in their treatment of these characters.

If there is no lasting bitterness for Kenneth, the same cannot be said of Terry and Brenda who, in a sense, collude in the 'plot' to put Debbie down. At one point, Terry acknowledges a communication with

Debbie, but despite all his talk of 'life, values, truth and all that jazz' we are left in no doubt as to the depth of his rejection — 'they used to ditch kids like Debbie on frosty hillsides and that would have been okay with me' (p. 81). And Brenda confirms — 'Eventually we (Terry and she) faced up to the fact that we loathed the sight of Debbie'. Their rejection, however, is not fully explained, and the author expects us to accept it as an inevitable outcome of factors inherent in the circumstances. We just have to take the author's word for it that what happened in the early years at home was sufficiently traumatic to have resulted in these entrenched attitudes. So Debbie did once get hold of Terry's O-level books and 'ripped them and smeared them all over with her filth', but similar things happened to Douglas in *The October Child* without leading to this permanent hardening of attitude.

The books can also be contrasted with respect to the treatment of the parents. Debbie's mother is only thinly sketched, but enough of her comes through to recognise the mother-who-has-given-up stereotype. She is worn down, pill dependent, living in a house which has become dirty and unkempt, neglectful of her other children and her husband, who eventually looks for an escape route.

Debbie's father is a high-ranking social worker who is always away on business. Unlike Carl's father, he does opt out, but in addition, in keeping with the sensationalist, melodramatic, TV crime-series nature of the story, he is portrayed as having a twisted and misguided approach to deviance generally — a typical trendy social worker who uses progressive rhetoric to justify attitudes which are not only out of touch with reality, but positively harmful, even criminal. For example, he supports the view that the seriously disturbed should be cared for in the community rather than locked up in institutions. Not such a radical view one might suppose, but not one with which the sensible, down to earth family doctor agrees — 'if you're interested in my opinion, that child should have been admitted to an institution years ago'. In fact, we are asked to believe that this father was in a sense responsible for his daughter's death. Inspector Bates is the rational, objective person with sound common-sense opinions. He knows, unlike Debbie's father, that killers like McKinley (who is suspected of killing four crippled children!) should not be let loose on the community, yet this father has actually encouraged him to relate to one of his own children as part of the rehabilitation process and has expressed the view that McKinley 'whatever his past problems has proved himself capable of forming and sustaining a fruitful relationship with the child' (i.e. Debbie). We are being encouraged to agree with Bates that father is totally misguided, but in the context of a story written by an author whose view of social workers is clearly superficial and prejudiced, even though we dislike father, we are not persuaded to generalise the argument to all progressive social work.

Summary

There is an attempt in most of the books discussed in this chapter to convey a sense of the harsh realities of family life where one child is severely disabled. Most of the authors would support the view that such subject matter is within the intellectual and emotional range of children, and by shielding children from it one could justifiably be accused of being patronising and overprotective. It is important for them to know the darker as well as the lighter side of living with handicap, and it is wrong to perpetuate the myths and errors, the sentimental and romantic accounts of a previous era. These are aims with which this author concurs. However, having made this point, it is important to recognise that some attempts to portray harshness are in bad taste and show an insensitivity on the part of the author to the needs of a child or adolescent audience. Brown, in *The Siblings*, attempts to capture the interest of the young reader by highlighting the extremes of behaviour associated with severe disability in such a way that the 'horror' of it all is the main hook. The disabled child is portrayed as a sinister figure, not possessed by the devil exactly, but behaving so outrageously and anti-socially that other people feel threatened and even frightened. The author's ambition appears to be to write a horror story rather than to genuinely explore attitudes towards disability. Similarly, in *Unleaving* the author is so intent on not pulling any punches that she goes further than necessary in her portrait of the severity and hopelessness of the disability.

The compassionate books in this collection — like *Welcome Home, Jellybean* — manage to combine a 'tell it the way it is' approach with a subtlety and humour in the writing appropriate to the sensitivities and experience of the age group. When reading these books we really do feel that the author has not refrained from writing about difficult topics, e.g. self injury, the mother's emotional state, the complexity of the sibling's feelings, but in a way that leaves us with a sense of the meaningfulness of the human life described and a feeling that the characters have survived, despite having had to cope with enormous problems. There has been a struggle for life which the characters are beginning to win.

This is not to say, of course, that these books do not have their contradictions in terms of integrationist philosophy, which are revealed if we look closely for example at the way some of the minor characters are treated or at the assumptions about the nature of adolescent identity struggles underpinning the thoughts and actions of the characters. These points will be taken up again later.

3   THE STRUGGLE TO BE MYSELF

In Chapter 2 we saw families with their backs against the wall trying to cope with severely disabled children who were at best a disruptive influence, and at worst perceived as a threat to the psychological survival of family members. In the books discussed in this chapter the emphasis is not so much on the effects of the child on the family as on the impact of the family on the growth and development of the disabled child. They are in some ways typical of a genre of children's fiction where there is a child character struggling for independence in oppressive family circumstances. The disability, of course, makes the child even more dependent, and provides an excuse for even more domination by the parents.

Domination can take various forms – it can be overtly coercive when the father, for example, lays down the law from a great height and a very loud voice; or it can be more subtle when the parents hide their rejection under gushing sentiment. The former represents the more traditional approach in books for children. The latter, for obvious reasons, is more difficult to convey, yet so much oppression experienced by disabled children is of this type that it cannot be ignored.

These subtle forms of oppression are in some ways more heinous than those which are more openly cruel and abusive. The so called 'normal' family is only superficially harmonious and growth-facilitating. On closer inspection, all kinds of negative attitudes and relationships can be detected and the child in particular feels the brunt of these. Overtly caring behaviour on the part of the mother can conceal a fundamental rejection of one or more of her children, and an approach to parenthood which seems open and permissive can in reality deny the child sufficient psychological space to develop his or her own personality.

All this, of course, can be overstated and often has been in the case of parents of disabled children. Commentators and researchers have been ready to detect faulty attitudes in these parents and as Thomas (1982) has pointed out 'parents of handicapped children have been the subject of simplistic concepts like "guilt" and "over-protectiveness" ' (p. 117). Nevertheless, it seems to me that any one who has experienced family life as a child and/or parent must recognise that, to put it simply, an outsider cannot always judge from appearances the true nature of family relationships, or at least certainly not from first or even second impressions; and it is often the case that what appears to be 'love' is only an act tricked up, either consciously or unconsciously, to fool the observer. I shall discuss a novel which deals with this form of family oppression later in the chapter, but to begin with I want to look at one in which the disabled heroine's struggle for survival takes place in a more traditional patriarchal family context.

The Fall Of The Old Regime

In M.E. Allan's *The View Beyond My Father*, the parents of Mary Anne are portrayed as almost totally insensitive to the needs of a daughter who has always had an eye defect and finally goes blind just before her thirteenth birthday. The book is set in the 1930s, but the issues raised are by no means out of date, particularly at a time when there is much talk of a return to Victorian values. It is in fact a timely reminder of just what such values mean for family relationships. Father is the great patriarch, who dominates the family, reduces his wife to dependency, and smothers his daughters with his version of love and affection. Although he finds his daughter's defect an embarrassment, he is determined to devote his life to her which for him means watching her every movement, keeping her from venturing forth into the world on her own, and generally restricting her. Her mother has very little say in the family affairs, although her whims are indulged and she is allowed to hire and fire maids, which she does frequently. She is a snobbish, shallow, egocentric person who really prefers being over in the big city buying clothes or gossiping in tea shops to bringing up her own daughters. Mary Anne finds her a 'bit silly' and a woman 'who had no idea what it was like not to see very well'.

This portrayal of mother is important because it provides Mary Anne with a negative model, precisely the sort of person that she does not want to grow up to be like. The parents are backed up by a Granny — father's mother — who talks about God making Mary Anne go blind for some higher purpose and who treats her like a four-year-old, and a 'stupid' teacher from a local low-achieving, girls' private school, who is her tutor.

It is no wonder therefore that even before she goes blind she has retreated into a secret world of the imagination and has developed a secret self. As she tells Dennis Weston, the boy she meets when for once she is allowed out for a walk on her own, 'They think of me as

a child and children aren't people to them.' Her feelings of oppression
are compounded by the fact that she is a female child living in a patriarchal family in a period when the roles disabled people, children and
women were expected to play rendered them inferior and dependent.
Her struggle to break free of all this is what the book is about.

One of the strengths of the book is the clarity with which it portrays
a young girl's growing awareness of alternative world views in a period
of social and political change. The starting point for Mary Anne is the
comparison of her father's attitude to her disability with that of the
surgeon who restores her sight, and others like the Weston family whom
she has befriended. The author's arguments are convincing precisely
because she grounds them in this experience of different people's
reactions to her disability. The reader is not being asked to compare
philosophical abstractions, but to see for herself, so to speak, just how
different social and political positions have different implications for
those always on the receiving end, like the disabled.

In sympathising with Mary Anne we find it hard not to agree that
the progressive views of the surgeon and the Westons are distinctly
preferable to the Victorian attitude of her father. A possible criticism
here is that the author has presented her argument in a form that is
too black and white. Her father is portrayed as just too reactionary
and authoritarian. Thus the surgeon describes him as a man who has not
'much imagination or psychological knowledge . . . a Victorian in his
views'. He also characterises him as a 'business type' who is 'dominat-
ing' and has a poor attitude towards children — 'I haven't any children
. . . but if I had, I hope I would treat them like human beings.'

This Victorian view is further characterised as simplistic and chauvin-
ist. Mary Anne becomes aware of this after her conversations with
Dennis and his father, whose general approach is in marked contrast to
that of her own father.

'Dr. Weston, on the other hand, had a very quiet voice, rather like
his son's and I always longed for more conversation with him.
Between him and Dennis I was starting to be thoroughly aware that
there were other views of life than my father's which, put simply,
were . . . well, simple. The British Empire was all that was important.
Everyone had to be Protestant, but not too ardently; one paid one's
bills promptly, and saved for the future. In spite of going to South
America and being able to speak Spanish quite well, my father
utterly distrusted and despised foreigners. He hadn't the least doubt
that God smiled on us all just because we were British. (p. 36).

However, it seems to me that there is nothing in this representation of a world view which is particularly inaccurate. In fact, the author by linking the 'personal' (the psychology of the father) with the 'political' (his political ideology) has provided a sketch of a person's outlook on life which, though written simply enough for children to understand, is more sophisticated than many others one can recall which concentrate only on one or other of these aspects. Of course, the author is not trying to present a BBC-type 'balanced' view. To have done so in this context would in any case have been inappropriate because presumably from our vantage point in the 1980s there is not much to disagree with as far as the principles espoused by the progressives of the period are concerned, and it goes without saying that the surgeon's optimism would probably appeal to most of us:

'Ideas are changing, especially attitudes to women and children. It may be a long, long time before women are treated as full human beings. I'm no prophet, but I give it fifty years to go. But it will come. Women got the vote but not much else. And children are human beings, too. There are people in the world who are beginning to realise that. The day may come when they have rights.' (p. 62)

One should also recognise that in any case ultimately her father does show a spark of humanity and is clearly not an irredeemable character. When Mary Anne finally confronts him on her return from Wales, he softens. This is the climax of the book, and in the build up to it the author demonstrates how the changing consciousness of the heroine results in positive action. The portrayal of her psychology here is interesting: as a disabled and oppressed person herself Mary Anne can readily understand the oppression felt by others even when they are not disabled. This is an optimistic view of disabled people's capacity for altruism. One is reminded of the well known deaf and blind woman, Helen Keller, who in addition to helping those with a similar problem to herself was passionately concerned with social justice, freedom and the rights of women (Lash, 1980).

Mary Anne's sense of her own oppression enables her to sympathise with Gwyn, whose condition she sees as much worse than her own. The attitudes towards the maids in the Agnus household are what you might expect of an upper-middle-class family of the times. If they stepped out of line they were dismissed immediately on the say-so of a mother exercising one of her few powers to influence father's decisions. Maids were non-persons, chattels, bottom in the pecking order whom the daughters of the household shouldn't get 'too thick with'. This was Mrs. Agnus's advice to Mary Anne, when she sensed that she was beginning to use the new maid Gwyn as a confidante.

When Gwyn learns of the pit disaster in her village, Mary Anne, on her own initiative, arranges for her to travel down to Wales immediately, accompanies her and returns on her own to confront her father. We feel that it is her experiences in Wales — her first-hand impression of life and death in the working-class community, the sympathy this invokes in her and the final comment of the widowed Mrs Powrys that Gwyn, her daughter, will need her job more than ever now — which adds the final stiffening to her resolve that her father must be confronted.

Her father's response to all this is predictable. He has, of course, been worried to death. He feels that she has been thoughtless and ungrateful and that there was no need to accompany Gwyn because the girl was used to travelling by herself. When he adds the inevitable 'your mother will want to dismiss her, and she will be quite right' this is enough for Mary. She is angry but remains calm, looks him straight in the eye and coolly and as clearly as she can explains that Gwyn's father and forty-eight others are entombed in the mine, that the family is poorer than ever and that Gwyn will be back the day after tomorrow. She then delivers her ultimatum — 'If you let my mother dismiss her I'll never respect you again, ever.'

Then in a crucial sequence, she achieves her emancipation.

Silence fell. My father gradually seemed to regain composure. We eyed each other and it was he who drew back.

'All dead?' he said slowly, at last. 'I didn't know. I didn't buy an evening paper. That's bad . . . that's very bad.'

'Yes,' I said, thinking of the stricken faces, the machinery of the mine black against the October sky.

'Well,' he gestured awkwardly around the kitchen, 'I expect you're hungry. Can you find something? Can you manage on your own? I had a boiled egg.'

'Of course,' I said. I had watched Gwyn carefully, feeling I might need to know one day. 'I'll have a boiled egg too. And I'll put the table ready for the others when they get back. I could do scrambled eggs for them, I think.'

He went away without another word and the drawing room door closed. I put on my egg and, while it cooked, I drank a glass of milk. I still felt nothing much, but it began slowly to seep into my mind that I had won some big battle. With myself, maybe, rather than

with him.
That day I had seen so far beyond my father I had somehow become free . . . (p. 123)

In general, the appeal of the book lies in the convincing way the
author has managed to convey through the description of day-to-day
events a sense of the changing values of the times. Old-fashioned
attitudes towards disability are portrayed as part and parcel of the
old regime, inextricably bound up with the nature of family life in that
period and a reflection of the general oppression of the weak and
powerless by the strong and powerful. Unlike many books in this genre,
the struggle for independence of the adolescent heroine is not portrayed as some biologically based universal feature of 'growing up', but
is situated in a deftly sketched historical context where it is a part of
a progressive social movement. The book is optimistic because we can
see in Mary Anne's success the beginnings of a new and more enlightened social order taking shape − one where the downtrodden
and oppressed, the blind, women and the poor − are allowed equal
opportunity for self-realisation, and where superstition and ignorance
give way to materialism and science.

Mother as Liberal Poseur

The next book to be discussed makes an interesting contrast with
The View Beyond My Father. Whereas the latter is historically located
at a time when progressive opinion was only just beginning to make a
significant impact on national policies, Kerr's funny but sad *Dinky
Hocker Shoots Smack* is set in a period several decades later when it is
acknowledged even by many liberals and radicals that progressivism
had become a rhetoric mouthed by new types of powerful persons,
often more concerned with justifying their own existence than helping
the needy. Such rhetoric legitimated a new form of repression.
This is a typical end of the 1960s book; it was first published in
1972. The family dynamics portrayed are reminiscent of those described by the anti-psychiatrists of that period like R.D. Laing and
D. Cooper. A favourite notion of theirs was the 'double bind' family.
Peter Sedgwick (1972) has provided us with the following snapshot
of such a family, a composite derived from the anti-psychiatric literature.

Mr Doublebind is reported to be a shifty, spineless, passive father, impoverished and rigid in his mental processes and bewildered by tasks involving quite elementary social graces. In the enactment of the family drama he is constantly upstaged by his spouse, a domineering dragon of a woman who sets unrealizable demands on the life style of her children and is then insecurely reproachful to them when they fail to live up to her immature stereotypes. The suffocating, spiky embrace of Mrs Doublebind, her tiresome niggling obsession with conventional manners, her intellectual and emotional dishonesty and her incessant moral blackmail are all repeatedly documented in the literature. (p. 23)

Dinky Hocker is fourteen, fat and lethargic. Her mother is a lady bountiful who runs therapy groups for dope addicts, but has no understanding of her own daughter's problems and needs. She allows her no real independence. She sabotages the one relationship with a boy, P. John, that Dinky does develop. Although P. John is something of an authoritarian type, he is potentially 'good' for Dinky, not least because he is intent on helping her to diet. Although her mother refuses to allow Dinky to see P. John, he thinks enough of Dinky to send her a Christmas present — a copy of *Weight Watchers Cook Book* — but this only elicits a sarcastic 'Oh my my my my my. Isn't that romantic' from mother. Even her rather weak husband recognises that she has gone too far, but he and Dinky feel powerless to stop her. Dinky feels totally resigned to the fact that her mother can make her do things and she hasn't the will to resist.

She then goes on to embarrass Dinky by telling everyone about the gold watch that she had wanted to give P. John. This is done in the usual way of the double bind mother — the denial of the very thing that she was doing — 'I'm not trying to embarrass you. But you *and* your friends should appreciate the fact that I *do* know what's proper and what isn't.' And then the final stab when she portrays the Christmas present as indicative of Dinky's friend — 'and that's *all* he ever was, a friend' — being primarily interested not in her but in her weight problem (p. 100).

This is typical of mother's behaviour, and gradually we see Dinky giving in to her. She refuses at first to read the letter from P. John that her friend Tucker Woolf has brought for her. She returns to her previous identity of Dinky rather than be called by her real and more dignified name, Susan, which was how she was addressed by P. John. She again becomes preoccupied with bizarre happenings, and as she retreats into her own world still further, becomes obsessed with tropical fish as well as food. The book builds to a climax when P. John returns — a slimmer and reformed character — but Dinky is in a worse state than ever and doesn't want to know him. Seeing him, however, is enough to spark off in Dinky a final cry for help. While all the dignitaries and other members of the 'community' are at the Heights Samaritan Banquet where speeches are made in praise of the good works of Mrs Hocker, her daughter is outside covering the sidewalks, kerbstones, walls, sides of buildings, doors of cars in Day-Glo paint, in every size and colour, with the statement — Dinky Hocker Shoots Smack.

Her friends Tucker and Natalia try to persuade her to wash off the incriminating evidence, but Dinky is resigned to being found out by mother 'Because she has a way of ferreting out the truth — instantly . . . She has radar, second sight and a third eye.' (p. 150). She then turns on her friends — her only support — and she blames them for exposing her in her fat state to the new slimmed-down P. John, and accuses them of treachery. When Tucker says 'Goodnight, Susan,' her reply expresses her feeling that her nicer, better, dignified self, Susan, has gone forever — 'Susan . . . has been swallowed up and suffocated by the oily, solid substance in animal tissue; she has been strangled by suet.' (p. 153).

An interesting feature of the characterisation is that the 'double bind' parents are presented as regarding themselves as liberal and progressive. Thus, the notion of the difference between appearance and reality is formulated in this instance as the contrast between the progressive political views of the parents and their repressive attitude and behaviour towards their daughter at home. I feel the author has made a bold attempt to break with convention here. Such repressive parenting is typically, and in most cases correctly associated with reactionary views, but equally, the author perhaps is trying to tell us, even in allegedly the most liberal of families one should not assume that the public values espoused are translated into enlightened child-rearing practices.

Another point to note is the author's well-observed distinction between this schizophrenogenic family and the family of P. John, Dinky's boyfriend. P. John also comes from a radical, progressive background. He is another one who feels neglected by a radical, and also in his case famous parent, and his response is to react against his father's views and value everything that his father doesn't. He feels that his father cares more about his political friends and causes then he does about him. Finally, as a result of his experience at school he is politically transformed and becomes extremely left wing – a return to the family tradition. This reaction against, and then return to the fold suggests that the 'neglect', if it can be called that, is different in kind from that in the Hocker family and clearly not as damaging psychologically.

Tucker Woolf, the narrator of the story, also has problems. He escapes into libraries and feels he is friendless, which is why he becomes so attached to his cat. Again, we see parents whose time is so taken up with their own careers – father losing his job and trying to start up a new business, mother with career aims in publishing – that the child tends to be neglected. A highlight of the book is his gentle and moving relationship with Natalia, who has been to a special school to which she returns when life gets too much for her. But she and Tucker get together and are clearly good for each other. They discuss their mutual problems and help each other. They reach a stage when they can even become objective about the significant adults in their lives and begin to see things from a less egocentric viewpoint. Tucker is helped by Natalia's telling him her own tragic story which contains some remarkable insights:

> 'She [her mother] used to get migraines . . . a lot of things are psychosomatic. After my father killed himself, I couldn't talk for a long time. Then I could only talk if I rhymed . . .
> He went through a lot and I didn't realize it. I was just all full of myself, embarrassed because my mother had a mental illness, and worried that the kids were talking about me at school . . . He really loved my mother and he couldn't help her – and I couldn't help him, because I was so conceited.'
> 'Conceited?' Tucker said.
> 'Conceit masquerading as an inferiority complex,' Natalia said. 'If I'd really felt inferior, I wouldn't have devoted all my time to worrying over what kind of impression I was making. You have to be awfully conceited to concentrate on yourself day and night.'
> 'I never thought of that,' Tucker said. 'but it's true. In my own case, I didn't even have any idea my mother had any ambition to be anything but my mother . . . She wants to be something more important.' (pp. 130-1).

Tucker has clearly progressed emotionally and socially, and this is further reflected in the way he confidently takes Mr Hocker to task over Dinky, and is instrumental in her parents' coming round to thinking that maybe they were not meeting her needs after all. It is through Tucker that the critique of the progressive rhetoric of a poseur like Mrs Hocker is articulated, and his comments on the meaning of terms like 'community' help to situate the book in a broader political context. The following passage sums up the main critical thrust of the book:

> There were a lot of freaky things about that spring.
> One was all the dope addicts pouring into DRI. Many of them were veterans the Army wasn't helping. Sometimes DRI couldn't even help them. The freaky thing about it was that they'd re-enlist, because it was easier to get dope in the Army than out.
> Even freakier was the fact that they'd all sit around complaining how dope had wrecked them, and then they'd go back to it. They were the saddest losers Tucker had ever encountered.
> It made Tucker think a lot about losing.
> He spent so much time around Mrs Hocker that he also began to think about this business of being a credit to the community.
> To Tucker's mind, things had somehow become reversed. The community ought to be a credit to the person, and not the other way around.
> It was the community that soldiers represented. If the community was all that right about war, the soldiers might feel less like losers.
> Most of the members of DRI were blacks and Puerto Ricans, all from poor families. They were all losing in the community.
> The community was a little like Mrs. Hocker: she meant well and everything, but she always seemed to be there after the damage was done. The best way to get Mrs. Hocker's attention was to get into some kind of trouble. (p. 141)

This book is written in a sharp, witty style and includes plenty of clever banter between the characters which is sometimes friendly and sometimes barbed, but always stimulating for the reader. Unfortunately, the story ends rather too abruptly. The Hockers go off to Europe as reformed parents apparently doing everything they can to 'show Susan how much they love her', but the family relationships seem too sick for a cure to be that easy. The author seems to have suddenly thought that the book should end on a happy note, but the reader is not convinced. In fact, Dinky herself is not just an unloved and stunted personality, but one who seems to have developed as a person with a serious problem who is just about to withdraw completely from reality. Mrs Hocker is a typical 'double bind' mother – one who overtly fosters independence whilst denying its realisation by covertly encouraging the child to remain dependent. A crucial feature of the 'double bind' family is that superficially everything appears to be reasonably normal. Both parents seem to be caring and, from the point of view of the 'community', seem to be good parents. But the author lets us in on the secret as to their true nature very early on in the book. We can see how Dinky's experiences are repeatedly invalidated by mother, how she feels unable to defend herself against her, how she is reduced to perceiving herself and situations through her mother's eyes as if this were the only reality and finally conforms to her mother's identikit picture of her.

It is because we are not convinced that there can be an immediate resolution to Dinky's problem that we are left uncertain as to whether the book is basically optimistic or pessimistic. It is certainly optimistic about children, witness the way Tucker and Natalia help each other and the efforts P. John makes to help Dinky diet. But it is generally pessimistic about adults in a way that *The View Beyond My Father* is not. One is reminded here of Geoffrey Fox's (1971) comments on the books of the well-known children's novelist Ivan Southall.

> I have been left with the sense that the writer has offered us a picture which is at once – awkwardly – both optimistic and pessimistic. Optimistic in that he shows us children placed in severely demanding circumstances through which learning, growth and change take place. The children are often profoundly wise; wiser indeed than their parents or teachers. For pessimistically the adults of the novels give little evidence of any capacity for growth and change: except for that forced upon them by their children. (p. 53)

It seems to me that, although this point should certainly be taken seriously, the book can be defended on the grounds that in the particular historical period in which it is set it may have been the case that parents were more out of touch with events, both locally and at world level, than their children. The long passage quoted above on the nature of 'community' testifies to this. Of course, one could argue that not all adults even in such a period would be so out of touch that their perceptions would be less accurate than those of their children. But even if there is only some grain of truth in the assertion, then this is enough to justify the author's stance. Since this inferior status for adults is not intended to be true for all time, we can be optimistic that the rising generation will not allow themselves to be so blinkered.

Policemen Are People Too

The same point, I think, can be made about an important novel by Ivan Southall to which I now turn. *Let The Balloon Go* is another novel where the central theme is the disabled hero's struggle to be himself, and where the presence of 'handicap' seems to bring the worst out in adults whether they be parents, doctors, neighbours, teachers or policemen. In this story mother does not figure much in the narrative, but she is there in the background as the archetypal overprotective mother of a disabled child. She is moody and changeable — 'A fellow never knew where he was with her' (p. 22) — often worried, anxious, tired and distressed, as she tries to cope with a twelve-year-old cerebral palsied son (John Clement) in addition to doing a part-time lecturing job. Her overprotectiveness puts her under even more pressure. She is less understanding of John's needs than father, but, as she points out, his job is such that he is out at work all day and does not have the same responsibility for John day in and day out. Neither parent, however, is very appreciative of John's perspective. The way they talk to him reflects their lack of insight and he knows this. They try to explain to him, for example, that although his body stops him doing activities that other boys of his age do, his compensation should be that he can do it all in his imagination. But this cuts no ice with John:

'How stupid it was, all those grown-up words, all those grown-up meanings. How could they expect me to *like* it?' Even when they were telling him about the things he could do they were saying it in such a way that the fun was about as joyful as a stab of toothache. And when he did use his imagination, as they said he should, someone would end up shouting, 'John Clement Summer, your imagination will be the death of me.' (p. 34)

Even the consultant, a Mr Robert Macleod, does not inspire confidence. Unlike the doctor in *The View Beyond My Father*, his words do not give the impression of someone in tune with the aspirations of the modern generation. Instead he is given to making claims which even John realises are, to say the least, suspect — 'I do know what goes on inside the mind of a handicapped boy, just as other men, the surgeons, knows what goes on inside your body.' Macleod talks to him about the possibility of an operation, but is incapable of treating him as an intelligent twelve-year-old:

'What will they do inside my leg?'
'I have told you a snip here and a snip there and things of that nature. Nothing you have to worry about. You'll never see it nor will anyone else. Your mother and father will fill you in on the details when you're old enough to understand.'
'I'm old enough to understand now.'
'I say you're not.' (pp. 36-7)

John is rarely left on his own at home, but when he is he is certainly not content just to sit there using his imagination. He decides that for once he will do something he really wants to do — something which he knows his parents would disapprove of. The task he sets himself is to climb a tree, like other boys do. It is effort enough merely to get the ladder up against the tree, but he eventually does this and after a gigantic struggle climbs the tree and sits triumphantly on one of the upper branches. When neighbours see him up there they immediately conclude that he should be brought down. The parents are still away. A policeman is called to climb the tree and effect a rescue.

It is the interaction between the policeman and John (pp. 94-106), which is the high point of the book, and it is worth looking at the author's treatment of this a little more closely. Up until this point John's confrontations with adults have been pretty one-sided reflecting his dependence on them, but up in the tree John finds himself in a position where for once he can dictate the terms.

At first Constable Baird seems to be making a good job of it. Baird is a neighbourhood bobby who clearly knows how to establish rapport with a kid up a tree — a spastic kid at that. He has done this sort of thing before and does not need any advice, especially not from John himself who at one point suggests that he should take his boots off.

'I was climbing trees before you were born' is his response. However, it is not as easy a task as he imagined. It is raining and he is sweating. John, who had previously insisted that the crowd of onlookers should go away, gets an assurance from Baird that they had been sent far enough away not to be able to see or hear anything.

Baird admits finally that he is too heavy to reach John's position — 'I guess a boy can go where a man can't. I'm licked, John. You're the king.' He praises John — 'You've done a remarkable thing' —

and for him that's probably the end of the matter as far as John's proving something is concerned, but remarkably, and this is the most important shift in the dialogue, John presses home his advantage, doesn't accept the policeman's suggestion that he should hang on for half an hour, and tells him he wants to get down by himself. This is too much for the policeman, who when thus confronted suddenly changes from a friendly, kid-loving policeman to a desperate, weak adult. 'That's not fair,' he says rather childishly. It isn't fair because it is his responsibility to make John safe because that's 'the sort of thing that happens to policemen all the time,' and at this point the rapport he has established breaks down and the conversation turns rather nasty. 'You do as I say, you little devil. I'm risking my life for you.' He then shouts down to the people asking someone to fetch the Rescue Squad. This is a mistake, because it means that John realises he has been told a lie; the people *could* hear even if they could not see. Baird recognises his mistake, and is remorseful, but it's too late because this betrayal seems to stiffen John's resolve to do what he wants to do. Why, after all, should he listen to a policeman who loses his temper, and lies? Moreover, the policeman's attitude is changing mainly due to the pressure from the crowd, who have their own idea of what a policeman should do. His identity as a policeman is under threat. 'It was the crowd below that made it so hard but the crowd would not go.'

And it is the crowd that provokes him into making another mistake. As John, against Baird's advice, starts swinging from branch to branch, the policeman blurts out − 'You must go back, John. Anybody can climb a tree. It's the getting down that's tough.' This is just about the worst thing he could have said: 'It was a dirty thing to say. If Constable Baird had struck him he couldn't have hurt more.' (p. 104).

But it makes John even more determined. Not only does he carry on with the task of getting down the tree, but on the way he even dares to help the policeman, whose foot has become wedged in the crease of a bough, by unlacing his boot for him! The final triumph!

Southall's portrayal of the policeman in this sequence is masterly. The man makes an attempt at 'impression management' (see Goffman, 1971) which fails. He is not a poseur, but he, like all of us perhaps, is worried about how his actions will be interpreted by others and what this will do for this self-image. However, he is to some extent powerless to alter the course of events. His outbursts have consequences. They sting John into further action, but the man has to continue playing the policeman role because the crowd expect it. This is a public place where individual identities are made or broken, and Baird has to retain his credibility.

It is this social psychological fact of life which Southall captures perfectly, and far from being pessimistic it is a demonstration of the humanity of adults. We do not condemn the policeman, but imagine that an era of self-doubt has begun for him. He might well join John's mother in saying 'For the life of me I don't know who's right; but I suppose I'll have to be wrong.' (p. 111).

There is also a point being made here about the nature of prejudice towards disabled children. It is not so much that people like the policeman harbour deep-seated, faulty attitudes, but rather that particular social situations precipitate people, sometimes even against the dictates of their own consciences, into striking attitudes and taking action which they might later regret. In a sense, the policeman has himself been disabled by his efforts to rescue John, and it is the conflict between his actual dependence at that moment and his desire to play the hero that produces the emotional state of which John receives the sticky end. This inner conflict is the result of the crowd's expectations as to what role he should be playing, and of his inability to meet those expectations, rather than a personality problem which the policeman 'possessed' before arriving on the scene.

These self-doubts that adults have are perhaps a routine feature of the human condition, but they become salient at a time of rapid social change. *Let The Balloon Go* (first published in 1968), has this in common with *Dinky Hocker Shoots Smack*. There is an implicit sense of the older generation being out of touch, and even a young disabled boy is aware of this in some degree. The emphasis on 'freedom' for the young is a reflection of the cultural preoccupation of the 1960s, and when John's father talks to him about this we suspect he echoes the thoughts of many other fathers of the period. 'What are you going to do with this freedom? Abuse it, as you abused it yesterday, or are you going to see it as the chance to say no to yourself instead of hearing it from others?' (p. 112).

Summary

The books have been reviewed in terms of how they represent the struggle for personal identity of disabled children in oppressive social circumstances. The focus is mainly on conflicts within the family, although adults outside the family are also involved. Allan's *The View Beyond My Father* is clearly located historically, and shows how attitudes towards a female child with a disability reflect different world views in a period of social and cultural reform. The book has a great deal to say about the relationship between disability, social class and the role of women and children at a time when Victorian values were losing their grip.

The historical context is also well defined in Kerr's *Dinky Hocker Shoots Smack*. The setting is America in the late 1960s early 1970s when oppression in families, particularly in that of Susan 'Dinky' Hocker, takes more subtle forms. The parents are allegedly liberals who, though actively involved in helping the deprived and the addicted, cannot see that their attitude towards their own daughter deprives her of self-respect and an independent existence. Southall's *Let The Balloon Go* is written for a younger age group, but conveys a similar message to Kerr's book.

In all these books the adults are portrayed as 'normal' but, in a sense, just as disabled as the children they are trying to help.

4 FRIENDSHIPS ACROSS THE DIVIDE

There are few simple statements one can make about the nature of societal divisions and how they relate to the life experience of disabled individuals. Yet it is obvious that such individuals will experience their disabilities differently depending on their location in the social structure. To ignore this is to ignore what may be the major part of the problem for a disabled person, which is that they suffer from more than one form of oppression (see Mehta, 1978; Wallace and Robson, 1971). Not only are they disabled, but they are also women, black, or members of a low social class, or they may be all four of these. Even being a child is also a form of oppression in some societies where the child-view is not appreciated.

One would expect authors, therefore, whose aim is to foster sympathy for and understanding of the disabled to be just as concerned with not in any way reinforcing the other divisions in society which are as equally oppressive for the disabled and non-disabled alike. In fact, if they are exploring the experience of disability in context some consideration of the other divisions is usually unavoidable, and therefore their books can be looked at in terms of how the interaction between disability and these other factors is treated. Some authors are more aware of the significance of this interaction than others. One such is Alan Marshall, author of *I Can Jump Puddles*.

A Question of Equality

In this autobiographical novel of a boy crippled by polio the hero's main preoccupation is achieving equality with his peers in the male-dominated, macho culture of the Australian countryside early this century. One's ambivalence arises because although we can support the celebration of the values of doggedness and self-reliance which enabled the boy to win through, his achievement is undoubtedly construed in terms of the sexist psychology of the times. Achieving equality with peers meant becoming a man. Becoming a man meant becoming like his father, and when it came to a straight comparison between his mother and father there was no doubt who was the more respected. 'When father visited me [i.e. in hospital] the conversation

54

was dominated by him even though he was a good listener, but with mother I always took charge.' (p. 44). He loves his mother, but he does not say what he respected about her in the way that he does frequently about his father. The following is typical:

> I respected men. I regarded them as capable of overcoming any difficulty, of possessing great courage. They could mend anything; they knew everything; they were strong and reliable. I looked forward to the time when I would grow up and be like them. (p. 25)

Manliness was defined as distinct from womanliness. Women tended to be more overtly emotional, whereas father never kissed him because men did not kiss boys. There was also a tendency for women to be less reliable than men. Thus, his mother surprised him on one occasion by referring to him as 'lame' — a word he detested for understandable reasons. Women were also in the main the characters who had the 'wrong' attitude to his disability. They were less likely than men to understand why he wanted to do things for himself, and were too ready with a helping hand like the matron in the hospital who could not see why he should want to tip his chair over in order to pick up some lollies that a boy had thrown him. Girls at school tended to be 'tell tales', and did not as a rule join in or even watch boys' fighting because this was considered too brutal for their genteel dispositions.

Yet to censor this on sexist grounds would be a simplistic and doctrinaire act. Sexism was part of the world-view of people living in Australia at that time, and the author's own attitude and that of other's towards his disability can only be understood in relation to this view. There were other aspects of the culture which were more progressive, and Marshall sketches in these as well. Man represented humanity in general, and was an expression of the independence and dignity of humanity, which was set against the view of humanity as weakly and dependent on God. 'Men like father, I thought, were stronger than any God.' (p. 19). One of the reasons that he felt from a very early age that he should take charge of his own life was that his father had taught him that God could not be relied on. Manliness was contrasted with womanliness, but it was many other things besides; like not kowtowing to people just because they were in a higher social class. In fact, there was an egalitarian thrust to the concept which suggested that although so many were weak or stupid or cowardly, there was a potential in all men to be manly irrespective of the class from which they came or the disability with which they were encumbered. There was a fundamental equality between men, and all men had the right to be treated as if they were equal provided they showed that they were willing to engage with life and develop their potential. The young Marshall, of course, was not fully aware of this philosophy, but he understood bits of it:

> I could easily have withdrawn from such battles . . . But if I had done these things I would never have been able to preserve an equality with them. I would always have been an onlooker, a victim of an attitude they reserved for girls . . .
>
> I was never conscious of any reasoning behind my actions nor was I aware that I was directed by motives designed to give me equality. (p. 163)

Moreover, self-reliance and forthrightness were not the only aspects of character which were valued. In the Preface to the Penguin edition Marshall refers to an additional value — compassion. (It is also interesting to note that in the same paragraph he refers to men *and women*.) In the text itself, we learn that compassion was more likely to exist as a value guiding action amongst the poor rather than the rich, i.e. amongst the swagmen and bushmen, and the reason for this was due in no small measure to the hard lives they themselves led. It was a compassion without pity:

> I liked these men because they never pitied me. They gave me confidence. In the world they travelled, being on crutches was not as bad as sleeping out in the rain or walking with your toes on the ground, or longing for a drink you had no money to buy. They saw nothing but the track ahead of them; they saw brighter things ahead of me. (p. 169)

These men did not patronise him like other adults often did, particularly those who looked at him in stereotypal terms. The bravery stereotype was particularly annoying. When he was in hospital adult visitors would bend over him and say that he was a brave boy, which used to embarrass as well as annoy him because he felt that he had not earned their tributes. His objections to adults patronising attitudes was something he shared with other children. Like others, he was often regarded by adults — men as well as women — as uninteresting and not capable of making a worthy contribution to the conversation. It was part of his own emergent sense of compassion that he could see that the attitudes of adults towards him were as much their problem as his:

> I saw with wonder that there were tears in her eyes and I wanted to comfort her, to tell her I was sorry for her. I wanted to give her a present, something that would make her smile and bring her happiness. I saw so much of this sadness in grown ups who talked to me. No matter what I said I could not share my happiness with them. They cling to their sorrow. I will never see a reason for it. (p. 230)

And so genuine compassion for a disabled boy was difficult for many adults to achieve in the context of the times. It was only men like his father and those at the bottom of the heap who managed it. The faulty attitudes towards the disabled were a feature of a hierarchically organised society, where the people at the top could only pity the disabled because they could obviously not see 'brighter things ahead' for them, and if they happened to be children then they were even more patronised. One could argue, of course, that women too were the objects of similar oppressive attitudes, but the boy Marshall cannot see this because for him women were frequently amongst those who were the most patronising and least understanding of his independence needs.

Alan Marshall's relationships with other children, then, must be seen in this context. It is mostly to boys that his endeavours to prove himself equal are addressed, and with one or two exceptions there is a tendency for girls to remain in the background. On the whole his efforts are successful and he is accepted as one of the boys. They treat him as an equal because he demonstrates repeatedly that he shares their values and can see the importance of sticking up for himself and handling himself well in a fight. In fact, his insistence that he be judged as they would judge any other leads him into some tricky situations. Rather than avoid the school bully he would go out of his way to needle, even to threaten him as with statements like — 'I'll fix you in a minute'. On one occasion he is required to make good his threats and challenges the bully to a fight with sticks in which he comes out on top, thanks to the choice of weapons.

This successful struggle for equality is credible in Alan Marshall's case because, apart from his paralysis, he has a lot going for him in personality and social-background terms. He is also intelligent and capable of doing well in school, even though he mucks about with the naughtiest of them and proves himself amongst his peers by standing up to the teachers and developing a disdainful attitude towards being caned. Thus, the physical nature of the divide between himself and peers did not prevent him from participating in 'pupil culture' (see Woods, 1980, p. 19). It is when the divide is 'mental', that is to do with large intelligence differences between the disabled and 'normals', that achieving the sort of equality that Alan Marshall does is much more difficult — difficult but not impossible. Clearly, a child who was rather slow could not have done all the things that Alan Marshall did which so appealed to his mates, but there is no inherent reason why he or she should not learn to participate as a valued member of a community of peers, as someone who could join in the fun, who was not a liability, who was different only in the sense that all individuals are different and who could even take initiatives rather than always being an observer of other children's actions. A book which portrays a slow-learning boy doing just this is Patricia Wrightson's *I Own the Racecourse*.

The World Turned Upside Down

This is the story of a slow and immature boy who purchases a racecourse for three dollars from an old man. His mates think that he has been taken for a ride, but Andy remains convinced that he owns the racecourse. His belief is reinforced by various work-people at the racecourse who go along with the idea, to the astonishment of Andy's mates, who become increasingly worried that the whole thing is getting out of hand. His mates are worried, and demonstrate their protective but perhaps slightly patronising attitude between Andy. Matt had tried to 'talk sense' to Andy — poor old Andy — but had failed. Mike, like the others, is worried because 'it seemed to him that the cruellest part of this whole cruel trick was that Andy should be made to look a fool — Andy who could not help himself and would never hurt anyone else' (p. 5). Joe had the idea that they should try to keep him away from the racecourse until he forgot his obsession, but the plan does not work because Andy is always one jump ahead of them. His enterprises are so successful that he even manages to get some of his mates in to the ground free, and on the occasion of Joe's birthday actually arranges a party in one of the stands!

A positive feature of this novel is the portrayal of a slow-learning boy as someone who takes initiatives, as opposed to being characterised as a follower rather than a leader, and an 'easily led' follower at that.

Although his naïvety is obviously being exploited when he is persuaded to 'purchase' the racecourse, he shows remarkable ingenuity in obtaining the money in the first instance, and then in using his new position as 'owner' for the benefit of himself and his friends. We see his self-confidence grow as he performs remarkable feats.

The main task as his mates see it is to attempt to show him 'what was real and what was not', but in doing so they themselves are surprised about how far Andy can go in maintaining the fiction. There is a message here, perhaps, for all who assume that a slow-learning person's assessment of reality must always be inferior to a 'normal' person's, and that they are always 'wrong' and the latter 'right'. The reason they are surprised by Andy's success is that they have themselves a child's-eye view of adults which assumes that adults always adopt a sensible approach and usually tell children like Andy off for being silly. But the adults here are not as straight as this, and in a peculiar way Andy's naïve approach brings out features of adult behaviour which are contrary to common sense but authentic enough. Andy in his own way is testing the limits of the adult view of things, and his attitude is just as valid as the more cautious approach of his mates.

Eventually, Andy makes a couple of mistakes which have disastrous consequences. He paints some benches white, which ends in an unsuspecting band of musicians marching off with white stripes on their trousers; and he tightens up the hare track with spanners with the result that the hare goes haywire. Even at this stage, when his game is clearly coming to an end, his mates are themselves too 'childish' to perceive the elasticity of adult reality. They think he is now going to 'cop it' and feel powerless to protect him from the reality which is going to come crashing down on him, but the committee who run the racecourse are persuaded to be generous and sympathetic and they 'buy' back the course for 10 dollars! So instead of being exploited, as his mates feared he would be, Andy makes a profit from the affair.

This book can be compared with others like DeJong's *The Wheel on the School* (discussed in Chapter 8) in which there is a focus on the community of 'ordinary folk', and with the way a disabled hero plays a leading role in reinforcing community values. Andy Hoddel makes his contribution to the community and the community responds. All the staff at the racecourse — the drivers, the cleaners, the men on the turnstiles, the women in the stalls — rather than ridiculing him, enter into the spirit of things, and keep his dream of being an owner alive in a way which is enhancing for Andy and community life rather than exploitative. As one of Andy's mates remarks — 'all of them had slipped away out of reality into Andy Hoddel's dream'. In fact, rather than just tolerating him, the people who lived in the crowded terraces and worked on the racecourse were tickled pink when they heard about his purchase and were positively delighted by it. 'It was as if a happy chuckle ran through all the twisting streets.' After a time even Andy's most cynical friend Mike saw some value in the enterprise, even wondering if it was inevitable that the fiction would eventually end: 'it's doing Andy a lot of good. He's twice as good as he was. Even if it crashes, he might still be better than he was . . . Only I don't think it will crash. It's too strong.'

To the working people in the community Andy's claim to be owner seems to represent a topsy-turvyness which appeals to them. After all, why shouldn't he or for that matter any one of them or indeed all of them own the racecourse? Why shouldn't existing property relations be overturned? They know it is not for real, but it creates a magic moment for them. Moreover, although the fun aspect is always there, they are quite serious in their support for Andy. For example, they talk of striking if the authorities insist on Andy taking down the decorations which he had put up for a party in the old stand.

I Own the Racecourse and *I Can Jump Puddles* both paint a rosy and optimistic picture of the capacities of 'ordinary' people to respond to disability in children in a sympathetic and understanding way. They contrast markedly with the more jaundiced views of the working-class community represented in some other novels which purport to provide a sensitive portrayal of disability.

A Tale of Us and Them

Take, for example, Elizabeth Beresford's *The Four of Us*. A superficial reading might suggest that this had a similar community orientation to *I Own the Racecourse*. Ben and his mentally disabled brother Teddy Bates team up with a girl called Amy and a lovable old eccentric called Mr File in an effort to save their local pier. Mr File is a former cinema projectionist in love with film and theatre. He is an obstinate but kindly old individualist, full of nostalgia for days gone by when people went hiking and were generally active rather than the passive TV watchers they are today. The pier is owned by Mr Adams, father of Amy, who manages the supermarket where Mrs Bates works. He allows them to use the pier. Their inititative is rewarded when Mr

Plum — a dealer in high-class goods — agrees to purchase the pier and make it safe for people to sit in the theatre and watch the film show which the group plan to put on.

This is certainly a lively and fast-moving story which portrays the adults involved in a good light as facilitators of the children's project and unprejudiced by the fact of Teddy's involvement. Mr File in particular strikes up a good relationship with him. He is a man with an interest who clearly does not give a damn what people think of him and wants to get on with living his life in his own way. Such a character is open enough and sufficiently unaffected by the small mindedness which can sometimes exist amongst those integral rather than marginal to the neighbourhood community, to be accepting of anyone — gifted or backward — as long as they are prepared to muck in and get on with it.

Nevertheless, one wonders about the attitudes amongst the mass of passive TV watchers on the estate, and how they may have reacted to Teddy's disability and what hope for integration there is in the context of this rather dull and very ordinary neighbourhood. As Ben says, the street where he lives seems to him to be 'the dullest and most boring street' he'd ever seen in his life. It is this rather dismissive caricature of estate life which is the book's weakness, because in the final analysis it raises but leaves unanswered questions about the possibilities of participation of disabled youngsters in the communities of the television age as opposed to those of a past and largely irrecoverable world of cinemas and local piers. It is the adults in the background who live on the estate who should interest us as much as those in the foreground of the story like Mr File and the two businessmen, who are community conscious up to a point, but nevertheless distant from ordinary folk. It is their children who Ben refers to when he says he does not 'have any friends on the estate' and they are the people for whom there is no escape from the boring street. It is their attitudes to disability which ultimately are the most important from an integration viewpoint.

Relating to children on the estate should be seen as a major task for Ben and Teddy if there is a concern that they should participate in the life of the local community. The author tells us that Ben has no friends on the estate, but this is not portrayed as a problem. Is it all right, then, that the children are relatively isolated from their peers in the neighbourhood? The issue is left unexplained in the narrative. The author asks us to accept that Ben is quite happy playing with Teddy and is not bothered about not having friends on the estate. His concern for Teddy is laudable, but he seems too virtuous and uncomplaining to be true.

There seems to me to be a fundamental contradiction here. On the one hand we are encouraged to see mental disability in non-stereotypal terms. Teddy is portrayed as living a normal life actively engaged in making a contribution to a useful project alongside his brother and new-found friends. Yet on the other, this is done in a way which reinforces an equally pernicious stereotype of 'estate people' — that undifferentiated mass of TV-watchers. It is as if they were part of some boring even hostile environment which the disabled child should avoid rather than engage with.

The 'Hooligan' Element

According to the stereotype, people who live on 'estates' are usually either boring or they are the breeding ground for the 'hooligan' element. As Neil recognises in *Welcome Home, Jellybean* (p. 19) it is the East End bunch who all live in the same housing development who produce rough characters like Beefy.

Of course, the point is not that hooligans do not exist, nor that a child from the 'estate' would never persecute a child with a disability. It is rather than such elements are too often portrayed as coming from working-class backgrounds, large council estates or inner cities, and it is only rarely, as in books like *I Own the Racecourse*, that we see the more tender and charitable side of working people. There is a particularly offensive example of this crude characterisation in Allan's *The Flash Children* (pp. 112–14). This is a simple tale of three children Megan (six-years-old), Arthur (eleven) and Dilys (ten), whose family moves from an idyllic rural environment to one which is still rural but nearer to the harsh realities of an industrial and rather 'grim' part of Cheshire. At school they befriend Brian, a partially sighted boy whose father is attempting to restore the old manor house which the children stumble upon whilst playing. They ask if they can help with this project and their offer is accepted. Brian, a quiet but hard-working and intelligent boy, gradually comes out of his shell, and becomes a full participant in the group, making a positive contribution to the common endeavour. Everything seems to be going smoothly until a gang of 'hooligans' turn up on their motorbikes. These hooligans inevitably speak with northern working-class accents in the way that middle-class writers imagine that class to speak — 'Ee, there's going to be a right bad storm'. There is a clear intention here to associate 'bad' people with 'bad' speech, at the expense of mocking the language of those whose English reflects the colour and richness of the communities in which they live. None of the heroes and heroines of the story, of course, speak in this vulgar fashion. Their language is standard, hygienic and correct.

On Snobbery and Social Status

Books like *The Flash Children, The Four of Us* and to some extent *Welcome Home, Jellybean*, however, are well intentioned, and do not set out to justify, celebrate or otherwise to comment on the class system, even though the authors can be accused of insensitivity here. The same is not true of Gina Wilson's *A Friendship of Equals*. Superficially, the snobbery and class discrimination which form the backdrop to the relationship between a 'normal' girl and a physically disabled girl seems to be the object of criticism by the author, but a closer reading suggests that the class system is accepted as an unalterable fact of life.

This book is explicitly about social class, with the disability factor being used as the occasion for the development of a relationship across the class divide. The friendship in focus is that between Stella Boncastle, an upper-class girl who lives in the manor house and who has been crippled by polio, and Louise whose parents own the village shop. It is Louise's parents who make difficulties for them. The village grocer is a proud man who at first forbids Louise to have anything to do with the Boncastles because of his conviction that one should not seek anyone's charity. One should keep to one's proper station in life, even though, of course, he hopes by her own efforts his daughter can improve herself. He insists that Louise must go to a 'better' school than the local comprehensive, despite the fact that she is lonely and miserable at the 'better' school. He is a man who, in common with the rest of his class, believes in self-help rather than ruling-class patronage.

Stella's parents want her to go to boarding school, but the decision is delayed because of Stella's conviction that she is being sent away because of her disability — 'It's my legs. They offend you. Looking at me reminds you — makes you feel bad — I've heard you say.'

All Louise's friends want her to tell them about her visits to the manor — they're jealous, bitchy and envious and want a bit of gossip out of her. She doesn't want to gossip about her new-found friend, but she gives in under pressure partly because she needs their friendship.

Their image of life at the manor is based on fantasy and gossip – the drunken mother of Stella and Stella herself lurching and hobbling round the spooky manor house – but at root there is an inverse snobbery here. Louise says as much to one of her old friends. She is talking to Debbie about Stella, but her reference to 'us' embraces all those girls of the same social status as herself. 'It's all of us who are snobby really – bending over backwards to have nothing to do with the manor house' (p. 102). And her friend Debbie states this view clearly: 'Well, what would they want to do with Us? They've got their own pals. People the same as them. Rich people.' (p. 102).

The upper class, however, do not seem to be as bitchy even though, in their own way, they are just as snobby. Stella's mother, like many of her class, does not seem to know what all the fuss is about. 'Money isn't everything' she says to Louise when the latter tries to impress with talk of her own modest inheritance. And she is surprised as well as disappointed when in the end Louise turns down her offer of financial support to enable her to take up a place at a 'posh boarding school' with Stella. She cannot see why 'backgrounds' should make any difference, both Louise and her father know that in reality they do, and Louise knows that she will not fit in at this school.

The upper class are, in general, snobs, but Stella is an exception. She is not one of those 'privileged, unthinking snobs' who go to private schools, and the reason for this is that she has been separated from other members of her class because of her polio which gave her such a 'ghastly time'. Disability is seen here as a way of making a person more human and above class differences. As far as class is concerned there is a plague-on-both-your-houses approach as if somehow the lower classes were as much to blame for class oppression as the upper classes. In the end the message seems to be that all that one can expect are handshakes across the class divide rather than the abolition of the class system itself. Everyone seems to know their place, and it is the exceptions like Stella and Louise that prove the rule.

Even the enlightened Boncastle family seem to accept that social injustice is somehow inevitable – 'Life's still so unfair, you know' says Charlotte Boncastle when she is trying to persuade Louise's parents to let her go to the private school.

A preferable approach to social class and its interaction with disability is contained in Cookson's *Our John Willie*. After the 1852 mining disaster and the death of their father, Davy and his deaf-mute brother, John Willie, are without a job and therefore turned out of their tied cottage. They find shelter in the summer house of the mysterious but generous Miss Peamarsh who discovers them and takes them in. She has a dangerous secret in her past and is being blackmailed by her former servant, Potter.

Times are hard — there is much poverty, unemployment and sickness, and there are plenty of nasty characters. The Coxons are the nineteenth-century version of your typical hooligans. They are from the lower orders, but they do not represent them. When Davey and John Willie tangle with them, they know full well that not all of their 'own kind' are like that. The Coxons are obnoxious because they have no sense of solidarity with other members of their class. They rob their neighbours, do not join in strikes, and report people to the justices for stealing and the like. People like that clearly do not have any sympathy for 'deaf mutes'. But there are other more dignified characters from the working class, like Talbot, unemployed, ex-miner, a union man and blacklisted. When he spoke to Miss Peamarsh 'his manner was not that of a workman or a servant; although his voice was different from hers, it was as if he were speaking to an equal.' (p. 89).

Disability and the Race Divide

Finally, two books will be looked at which are concerned mainly with the interaction between race and disability. The first has been discussed extensively elsewhere (see below) and will not be dealt with at length here. It is mainly concerned with racial prejudice, but has a central character who is blind. Theodore Taylor's *The Cay* is a novel set in the Caribbean in the early days of World War II. A young white boy finds himself stranded on a raft with a seventy-year-old West Indian. Philip has inherited his mother's prejudice and bigotry, and at first is frightened of the black man whom he regards as ugly and stupid. Quite suddenly Philip goes blind as a result of a blow on the head, and is even more dependent on Timothy, the black man, in his struggle for survival. Timothy eventually dies protecting the 'young boss'.

The book has been the subject of controversy (see Baskin and Harris, 1977) on account of the way it reinforces the old image of the inferior black man giving his life for a racially superior person — a man, to use Taylor's own phrase in the Puffin edition, of 'primal instinct' who uses his pragmatically derived survival skills to help the potentially more civilised white child, just as the faithful old black nanny cherished and protected her white charges (see Dixon, 1977). Others have argued that the book can be read as a simple story of how a white child overcomes his prejudices and grows up to appreciate the humanity of black people. Timothy was caring towards him not because he was white, but because he was young and disabled. He calls him 'young boss' out of habit as an old black man in the 1940s probably would have done.

The second book is G. Kemp's *Gowie Corby Plays Chicken*. Gowie has emotional and behavioural problems, although he himself does not see it this way — 'I don't have problems or difficulties. I just have enemies' (p. 31). He expresses his anger by provoking other children, stealing from them and playing nasty tricks on them. Eventually he gets his come-uppance when the boys at school gang up on him and beat him up near his home. It is at this point he meets up with Rosie — a black American girl who has come to live next door. She helps him into the house and cleans him up. He senses her genuine concern for him and opens up to her about his fantasies (he thinks of himself as Count Dracula), his current concerns and his home background — his mother works at a club every night, his father walked out some time ago and is now in jail, his brother Mark is in reform school, and the older brother Joe was killed in a motorbike accident. Gradually, with Rosie's help, he begins to face up to his problems with a new confidence. He begins to settle down to school work. He starts to get on better with the teacher and the other pupils. His fantasies are constructively channelled.

This story contains a number of interesting aspects which relate to the theme addressed in this chapter. Communication across several divides is explored — between an emotionally troubled boy and a black girl, his peers at school both male and female and his teachers. Rosie's blackness tends to be underplayed, but towards the end of the book the author engages with the question of racism. Gowie's brother Mark returns from reform school and tries to make him promise that he will never go near that girl again, but Gowie defies him — 'I gotta say that girl has been kinder to me than anybody in my whole life, and she makes me laugh and she makes me feel good, so there.' (p. 112).

It is evidence of Gowie's transformation from a negative to a positive character that he can defend Rosie in this way. At the beginning of the story he is at risk, we feel in retrospect, of becoming even more of a racist than his brother. He is distrustful of liberal-minded teachers, thinks he has enemies and feels that 'you've gotter look after yourself in this stinkin' world' (p. 43). Children who think like that are not noted for their racial tolerance.

One's doubts about this book arise from a consideration of the treatment of the two main characters — Rosie and Gowie. Rosie is too much of a 'good angel' figure, and her appearance on the scene is somewhat contrived. She accepts Gowie at face value, and her reforming of him merely by the force of her own personality (but what is this?) lacks credibility. The cause of racial understanding is not helped by glamourising black characters any more than it is by vilifying them. The character of Gowie is also a problem. The author clearly intends him to be a reformed character by the end of this story, but is the evidence such as that mentioned in the previous paragraph sufficient to persuade the reader? In his unreformed state, Gowie is portrayed as a potential sadist as far as his treatment of a certain girl pupil is concerned. Heather is unpopular and a cry-baby. Gowie regards her as the 'stupidest female slob in the world', and imagines her 'being tortured in a deep dark dungeon'. At other times he describes her as a 'silly fat fool' with 'two left feet and no brain', and he takes a positive delight on one occasion in making her cry — 'I hear a little sob as I whistle into the bright morning, feeling at one with the world' (p. 44).

All this is understandable if we regard it as a reflection of his personal problems. But the reader may be shocked to learn towards the end that the author appears to be interpreting this behaviour as a slight exaggeration of a naughty boy's sense of fun and impishness, because even when he finally becomes more likeable, presumably to show us that he has not become a goody goody, she has him making practical jokes of which Heather is the main butt. We observe him letting mice out of the cage and smiling with delight at the pandemonium he causes. A harmless prank, perhaps, but in view of his previous vitriolic comments about her, the following leaves a nasty taste — 'I watch Heather fall flat on her face as she tries to stop one running under the table and this is a lovely sight' (p. 134).

I do not feel this is somehow put right when we learn on the final page that Gowie actually marries Heather, a typical Gene Kemp surprise package. Do we presume that he goes on persecuting her? Do his sadistic tendencies turn into sexual advances? If so, is that supposed to be where such tendencies lead in normal boys; surely, a conventional and sexist view of sexual development and one that almost excuses his early violence towards her?

Summary

In this chapter I have been concerned with books where disabled characters are observed interacting with others in social contexts where various forms of prejudice and discrimination are pervasive. Marshall's

I Can Jump Puddles is probably the richest in terms of number of themes explored and the subtlety and detail of the social and historical backcloth constructed. It contains a vivid account of a disabled hero's struggle for equality in the context of a male-dominated macho culture, where powerful figures like his father are forthright and independent but not without compassion, yet where the dominant view is undoubtedly sexist. It also includes some interesting observations on the positive attitudes towards disabled persons held by those on the lowest social rung in a hierarchical society, and the patronising attitudes of adults towards children in general and disabled children in particular.

Wrightston's *I Own the Racecourse* is a simpler book aimed at younger children. The hero is a slow-learning boy who does not have Alan Marshall's intellectual gifts, but who in his own way is just as capable of taking initiatives and participating in community life. The book raises some interesting questions about the perception of reality from different viewpoints. Like the 'normal' children in the story, the reader is made to feel that Andy's perception has its own validity, which gives him a certain dignity. This book shares with *I Can Jump Puddles* an optimistic view of the capacities of 'ordinary folk' to generate community spirit and to sympathise with and understand children with difficulties or disabilities.

In this latter respect both can be interpreted as contrasting with Beresford's *The Four of Us*, which paints a picture of 'ordinary folk' as a mass of passive TV-watchers who live in a very dull and ordinary neighbourhood, whose children do not mix with the disabled character or his brother, and who have to be persuaded to participate in community enterprises. The stereotype of 'estate people' here is matched by Allan's stereotype of the 'hooligan element' in *The Flash Children* and by Wilson's acceptance of the conventional wisdom that the class system is inevitable. Cookson's *Our John Willie* contains a more appropriate treatment of working-class characters.

Two books are discussed which deal with disability in the context of a racist society. Taylor's *The Cay* has been criticised for reinforcing the stereotype of a black person as culturally inferior, but it has been argued by some commentators that this criticism is not valid. Kemp's *Gowie Corby Plays Chicken* contains some interesting aspects, but the force of the book as an anti-racist text is reduced by the glamourisation of the leading characters.

5 WE ALL MAKE MISTAKES: LEARNING ABOUT DISABILITY

Children's novels can be looked at from the point of how they portray different forms of reaction amongst 'normal' children to their disabled peers. Some authors would agree with the notion that children tend to be less readily influenced than adults by expectations based on stereotypes. They would agree with the view put forward by one disabled woman: 'The children that I played with treated me as one of them . . . It was probably because when children are very young they don't notice that a disabled person is any different from anyone else.' (Campling, 1981). Alan Marshall had a similar experience 'Children make no distinction between the one who is lame and the one who has full use of his limbs. They will ask a boy on crutches to run here or there for them and complain when he is slow.' (*I Can Jump Puddles*, p. 78). Likewise, their sense of humour is not restricted by adults' tactfulness 'They often laughed at the spectacle of me on crutches and shouted with merriment when I fell over.' (p. 79).

But this surely is not every disabled person's experience? It is a commonplace that children can be cruel as well as kind, and the range of reactions amongst them is probably as diverse as it is amongst adults. What many authors try to do is convey this reality – to portray the variety of children's responses. Sometimes it is not just a question of 'good' and 'bad' attitudes but of mistaken approaches due to a failure of communication.

Faces in a Silent World

This latter point is interestingly explored in Veronica Robinson's *David in Silence*. David is a profoundly deaf boy who has moved to a new neighbourhood where he is regarded at first with curiosity. He is befriended by Michael, who plays with him but cannot prevent himself becoming bored with David's company at times. David's attempts to relate to other boys are not very successful. He joins in a game of football, but holds on to the ball for too long and shows off so much that the other boys begin to turn against him. There is no maliciousness involved and the boys are basically trying to be sympathetic, but they are at a loss to know what to do about David because they cannot communicate with him. Eventually, in an interaction sequence well observed by the author, their bafflement gives way to 'uncomfortable feelings' and then they become 'suspicious of him and afraid of themselves' (p. 65). Even at this stage we feel that perhaps the worst that can happen is that they'll probably refuse to play with David, but there is another twist which leads to further escalation of the conflict.

As David sat up and saw the boys around him talking, he looked from face to face trying to decipher what the fuss was about. They appeared to be angry. Was it with Paul for having knocked him down? He picked the face that was nearest him and which he could see most clearly. He watched the rapidly moving lips, desperately trying to read a sentence or even catch a word.

He saw the very slight heave of the chest for an aspirate, followed by the very narrowly opened lips, of the long E sound, and the drawing together to make an S — 'He's'. The next important word seemed easy — 'Good'. The only phrase he was able to lip-read had been in fact, 'He's a coot'. David did not know the word 'coot', and because the hard C and G and T and D look alike on the lips he read the sentence as 'He's good', and took this to refer to his playing. They thought he was a good football player, so he was prepared now to be generous. He picked up the ball and climbed to his feet.

'Eyar', he said, meaning 'There you are', and tossed the ball towards his captain almost with smugness.

At any other time the boys would have acknowledged that David did not realize what had happened; but in their present mood his cheery flippancy and self-satisfied gesture aggravated them all the more

'He wants to play!' one of them jeered. 'He can't hear. He can't hear. He makes noises like an animal.'

The creepiness was frightening. Fear, mistrust and ignorance combined to arouse the mob instinct in them and they drew close together. (p. 67)

The strength of this passage lies in the way it conveys succinctly all the elements which go to make up an act of discrimination and rejection. There is the misunderstanding on *both* sides, the casual way in which the situation gets out of hand, the insecurity and complex feelings of the boys, the animal metaphor and the influence of the group situation. The author also manages to get across a great deal of information about the experiences, behaviour and needs of deaf people. The latter, of course, is of great importance if one considers that the main cause of prejudice and discrimination is ignorance, i.e. a model of attitude which suggests that, in the main, the negative aspects flow from the misinterpretation of each other's actions due to lack of knowledge. In this book the information about deafness is well contextualised so that it only occasionally disrupts the flow of the narrative. It is mainly through the relationship between David and Michael that the reader learns most about deafness. Michael himself learns from David's brother Eric about how David can feel sounds by feeling vibrations on people's throats, and how he can lip read if you speak clearly and face him so that he can see your lips. He also learns how difficult it can be to relate to someone who is profoundly deaf.

But perhaps the most profound learning for the 'normal' peers is not about the facts of deafness which are peculiar to David, so much as about those aspects of David's achievements with which they can readily identify. When David is chased by the lads after the football match, he runs into a tunnel and in his panic falls into the water at one point. He drags himself out, but is so tired and disoriented that he heads in the wrong direction. He moves towards the 'face' at the end of the tunnel — the white circle of daylight which seems to take on a life of its own and becomes associated with his fears and recent events.

> With nothing else on which to focus his eyes, he watched the daylight ahead steadily, until out of the darkness it became distorted and appeared to jump about. He blinked, but the round light patch grew more and more like a face. He shut his eyes to blot out the vision and walked on, and where the face had been was now a dense black shape surrounded by a grey halo which moved up and down under his eyelids in time to his footsteps, but it was more like a bouncing football than a face. (p. 74)

At a later stage the face returns: 'The white circle of daylight was larger and more like a face which moved in time to his footsteps, a round, white blank face, that looked at him with hostility.' (p. 74).

At the end of the story when Michael and some of his friends go down the tunnel in a raft they also see these 'faces', it gives them the creeps and they realise that David must had have nerves of iron to cope with this. But Michael's insight goes deeper than the rest. He realises that it probably wasn't the faces he was frightened of so much as 'people not understanding him, people hunting him as if he were a fox or a hare' (p. 128). They leave the tunnel, each of them finding that their tentative liking for David had grown into admiration because he had been all the way through the tunnel and they had turned back. Children and adults for that matter come to an understanding of the disabled by going beyond their own first impressions based on appearances. People are not what they seem, and people with disabilities are too easily labelled as what they are not. These kinds of error are typical, but it is possible, as we have seen, even for children to develop profound insights into the world of a child with a disability. Michael and his mates manage to achieve this. As in many stories, however, there is a certain predictability about this development which is not to be disparaged, but which is typical of the way relationships are normally portrayed, with the 'normal' eventually understanding the 'abnormal'. A more original approach would have been to have looked at the way one disabled child might have perceived another, and how both might have perceived so-called 'normal' children. Such an approach may be based on a model derived from the common-sense view that children with disabilities have a greater chance of understanding other children with disabilities than 'normal' children have, and because they are sensitive to situations of unmet need are also more likely to appreciate the oppression experienced by many non-disabled children in our society.

Meeting the World Halfway

This is the starting point for J. Slepian's excellent portrayal of character in *The Alfred Summer*. This is a humourous book containing many simply expressed psychological insights and written in a lively and chatty style. Lester is a ten-year-old boy with a form of cerebral palsy who describes himself as being 'an expert in knowing what people say. They may not even know that they are saying it, but they are just the same' (p. 2). He certainly does not know everything about himself and life, but he is remarkably insightful for a ten-year-old. He refers to his mother as the

'half love, half-hate lady' [who] 'has to keep the old man's temper down because, get this, because somehow it's Her Fault that I'm this way. And along with this she has to keep the strings between us in good shape at all times. Actually, I do my share of keeping the strings attached I know. But the difference is I know they are there and she doesn't.' (p. 46)

In Lester the author has successfully managed to portray in simple language a central character who is disabled, has an extremely agile mind, a good sense of humour and is something of a psychologist and philosopher!

The story centres around the building of a boat which Myron, described as rather fat and clumsy, wants to build so that he can, according to Lester, 'sit in the middle of the ocean to get away from his lonely normal life' (p. 50). Of course, Lester's mother, whose judgements are always so impressionistic and superficial (which is the reason for Lester's hatred of people who judge from appearances), cannot see this is Myron's motivation and therefore because he seems normal — 'a good boy, a fine boy' — does not mind Lester playing with him. This is not true of Lester's brother — Alfred — who is on the slow side. Mother is at least perspective enough to realise this but it prevents her seeing him as a person — 'He's retarded can't you see that . . . leave him alone. He's not for you.' (p. 7). What she couldn't understand was why Lester liked him: ' Everyone he knew, his parents, Myron, his teachers, people on the streets, in the newspapers, Christ! the whole world was struggling. Struggling to have more, to be more fearful and striving. Except Alfred.' (p. 49).

The author's portrait of Alfred is sympathetic and insightful without being sentimental. It was his simplicity that made Alfred easy to understand, but it also provided him with an outlook on the world which was more accepting and in some ways more positive than his intellectual superiors. He could relate to Lester without being prejudiced by the latter's physical appearance. Alfred was one of the few people who saw his mind rather than his impaired body. Alfred and Lester are joined by Claire and all help Myron with his boat. The former become so keen to make a useful contribution that they even formulate a plan to steal some oarlocks from rowing boats in a public park. This is the first of a series of events that same afternoon which culminate in Lester's acting decisively and bravely when Alfred has an epileptic fit on the train going home. This experience confirms Lester's belief in himself. He realises that he can do things by himself and the strings tying him to his mother are finally broken. His father sees him for the first time as a 'mensch' (man).

But there is a note of sadness. Things do not really turn out too well for Alfred, and Lester senses the lack of hope in Alfred's mother's voice when she informs him of the nature of Alfred's condition. Alfred disappears from the scene, but we are invited to think of him being as pleased as punch when his mates decide to change the name of the boat from 'Get Away' to 'Alfred'.

The central psychological theme of the book, however, revolves around the issue of the relationship between self and appearance. Neither of Lester's parents can 'read' him properly. An important learning for Lester is that it is perhaps not enough just to be yourself and hope that other people will understand you, but you also have to be concerned with how you present yourself. In other words, to some extent he had to meet people halfway, and present himself in a way that gave other people, particularly those who judged by appearances, access to his true personality. The alternative was to be perpetually misunderstood and reduced to forever wallowing in self-pity. He is helped towards an understanding of this by Claire, who tells him of her 'aziff' theory

'people can see what you are by the way you act, not by the way you feel inside. You can act as if anything you want. And pretty soon the way you are on the outside becomes the way you feel inside. Get it? Aziff' (p. 69)

This puzzles Lester at first because putting on a front smacks of insincerity and lacks authenticity. It is precisely this way of judging people which he loathes. 'Lester felt full of protest. Wasn't that just what he hated? People judging you by your front? Wasn't he a good example of that?' (p. 69). This reaction helps Claire to elaborate her theory in a way which provides a useful lesson for Lester. It confused Claire, but then she told him her Aziff Theory must be for bad things about yourself you want to change . . . Even you could do with some change Lester.' (p. 69). He finally realises the germ of truth in her theory when he meets Frankie — an old man who has no voice box.

Here's her Aziff Theory in person. Here's the old guy not a bit sorry for himself. Or at least acting as if he isn't. And so no one feels sorry for him either. The opposite. He could be crying in his wine over himself. Instead, he's giving life a good kick in the pants. (p. 85)

The final demonstration of the theory in practice is at the book's climax when Myron, his famous boat sunk, confronts the jeering crowd, and instead of feeling oppressed by them and sorry for himself, stands before them, laughing and giving a victory wave, to which the crowd respond by laughing with him rather than at him.

Lester is clearly helped by these experiences to come to terms with himself and his own situation. One wonders, however, to what extent he himself did at any stage 'wallow in self pity'? He seems to give in to Claire's interpretation too easily. The interpersonal processes as described by Claire are interesting and insightful, but are only one side of the story, and one is inclined to agree with Lester's initial reaction that it is for other people to learn not to judge only by appearances, rather than for him to be over-concerned with his own front.

However, the book gains in depth by introducing these aspects of social psychology into the narrative. Many of the problems faced by all children — not just those with disabilities — are due to lack of experience in self-presentation techniques (see Goffman, 1971), and perhaps the message that it is not enough just to be yourself in a simplistic sense is a useful starting point for self-reflection and group discussion.

Another positive feature of this book is the way the insights do not all come from one character who possesses a monopoly of psychological knowledge and acts as the expert on human relationships. All the children learn a bit from each other. When this is not the case, we can be sure that the expert character will punctuate conversation in a way which deadens the narrative.

The Child as Secondhand Expert

I shall now consider two books which fall into this trap. L. Lamplugh's *Sean's Leap* is about a 'maladjusted' boy Sean who goes to Bramscott, a residential special school where Daniel's parents are teachers. He is an insecure, unhappy boy from a broken home, whose father has run off leaving a mother who can't cope with bringing up the children on her own. When he finds out that his mother is going to have another baby this becomes the final straw, because he knows it will mean a postponement of any plans to return him home. And so he decides to escape, not in order to go home but just to get away because he is so down in the dumps. He steals some money from Daniel and catches a boat to a small island off the coast. He is followed by Daniel and his friend Alex, who watch him get off the boat and then chase him across the island. At one point Sean leaps down a steep incline near the cliff edge and injures himself, and in getting help Daniel and Alex miss the boat back. Fortunately, the island's owner, Merlin, and some of his friends agree to put them up. Their stay on the island of three or four days is marked by a gradual change in Sean. At first he is a 'bloody nuisance'. At one point he tries to escape yet again, this time by taking a motor boat without permission. The adults react firmly but fairly and do not reject him. Even Alex, who is far less sympathetic than Daniel, comes round to looking at Sean in a more favourable light. Sean eventually makes a great leap forward emotionally, and by the end of the book is beginning to trust his new-found friends.

It is the character of Daniel which is problematic in this story. As the son of teachers at the residential school he has the background information on Sean. Unlike Alex he knows that the boys at the school are not 'dimwits' despite being backward in school work, and that 'almost all of them have had some sort of smash up at home'. He tells Janet (one of the friendly adults on the island) about Sean's background — 'there are several siblings in care' and explains Sean's recent behaviour — 'it's because his mother's just had another baby that Sean started going off last week'. When Sean is spooked by hearing a tape recording of some birds and Alex remarks on how he seemed to suddenly look like a much younger child, the wise Daniel provides us with the explanation — 'Perhaps in one way he still is. Perhaps a bit of him stuck there' (p. 108). He knows Sean's ways because he has seen it all before. He observes how he sulks 'like several of the Bramscott boys' when he has been told off by someone he liked. Alex, of course, doesn't have Daniel's experience, and his initial reaction is to become edgy with Sean. The adults, however, realise that he needs some sort of anchor.

Daniel is thus portrayed as the modern version of a too-good-to-be-true character. He is not so much a traditional voluntary worker motivated by pity, as a social worker whose understanding derives from expert knowledge. The explanations he uses are the stock explanations of social pathology (see Meighan, 1981, p. 323) — broken home, regression, insecurity, etc. — and rather than illuminate Sean's uniqueness merely serve to paint a crude picture of your typical maladjusted child. All this is unstimulating because it shuts down any attempt to explore motivation further. The main strength of fiction is precisely that it does not provide the definitive explanation, but can suggest through the narrative and the interaction of characters differences of viewpoint, ambiguity and a sense of the complexity of human relationships, even in novels written for children. *The Alfred Summer* achieves this. In

Sean's Leap the explanations are too pat and in the final analysis too patronising. Daniel's insights are not derived from personal experience, judgements on the basis of which would be more circumspect and tentative, but are merely secondhand interpretations, gleened from what he has picked up from his parents and professional workers. For example, on page 96 we learn that he remembers overhearing someone at Bramscott telling a visitor 'What most of these boys need is something to hold on to.' Sean is packaged up, then, by Daniel's looking at him as a social worker would. Daniel is the expert and appears to have no warts of his own. He is a figure with whom children would have difficulty in identifying.

The Child as Do-gooder

Another novel where the 'good' guys are portrayed as little experts is Allan's *The Flash Children* (see also pp. 62–3). Unlike Michael in *David in Silence*, who does on one occasion admit to being bored with the company of David, or Lester in *The Alfred Summer* who is full of self-doubt, the children of Allan's novel seem to be too saintly and, particularly Dilys, too all-knowing to be true. Dilys sounds more like some form of psychological case worker than even Daniel. We are told that she grew 'observant over Brian [the partially sighted boy] and knew he was clever', and even knew how he needed to behave to be accepted by others. Her discussions about Brian with his father are almost like a case conference:

'He wouldn't like it any better in a special school', Dilys said with such confidence that Mr Pelverden looked surprised.
'Did he say so?' 'Oh, of course not. But I think he's proud. He hates to be different and he is clever. Either way it will be . . . Well, hard for him. It's awful. But I – I think he'll manage in the end.'
'You are a very perceptive young lady'. said Mr Pelverden. (p. 56)

She adopts a similar attitude to a couple of tearaways – Dan and Edith. She knows that their mother has died and they are being looked after by an aunt who cannot manage them. When she, Megan and Arthur catch them teasing their cat amongst the reeds, she thinks they are really awful. However, she reflects on their situation and her diagnosis is that they probably behave like that because they are lonely. 'Some day I think we'll have to do something about them', and she eventually plans a successful intervention.

Dilys really is an unbelievable character. Her attitude is as patronising as the old-fashioned do-gooding approach to charity cases, as if she were somehow trying to 'save' Dan and Edith in the manner of a missionary. After all, they might grow up to be like the motorbike hooligans whose vandalism 'they might have aspired to when they were older, if they had not learned to work for a reason' (p. 110).

On another level this reflects a more general attitude which is compassionate towards young children from broken homes but not so towards such children when they are older, when they are dubbed 'hooligans' who are beyond the pale. There is no attempt in the narrative to examine the motivation of the 'hooligans', or to explore the reasons for the vandalism of property in the country by deprived sections of the community who live in inner-city areas.

Summary

The reactions of 'normal' children to their disabled peers take various forms. In Robinson's *David in Silence* the cause of the boys' rejection is located not so much in their attitudes as in the multiplicity of factors influencing the interactions between them and David, a profoundly deaf boy. Their prejudice is not so deep seated that it is not open to change in the light of their experiences of David. The book provides insights into the social-psychological dynamics of discrimination against and persecution of a disabled child. It shows how children can learn from their mistakes and arrive at a more mature understanding of disability.

A similar theme is taken up in Slepian's *The Alfred Summer*, but this is in some ways a more sophisticated book because it explores the inner life of the main disabled character with more subtlety, and provides insights into the social psychology of disability which are more profound.

In neither of these books is it the case that any one child possesses a monopoly of psychological knowledge. They all make mistakes whether 'normal' or disabled. Even the insightful Lester in *The Alfred Summer* realises that his past behaviour is open to criticism. Unfortunately, in some other books portraying children's reactions to disability this 'all in the same boat' approach is not evident.

In Lamplugh's *Sean's Leap* for example the narrator is a child whose parents teach at a special school and who is portrayed as possessing special knowledge about Sean, a 'maladjusted' boy. He is the knowing subject and Sean is the known object. In Allan's *The Flash Children* the do-gooding heroine is also portrayed as some kind of mini-expert. In neither case is the disabled character treated as a person with a valid view of the world.

6 ON THE 'DIAGNOSIS' AND 'TREATMENT' OF EMOTIONAL AND LEARNING DIFFICULTIES

The scare quotes in the title reflect one's caution in using such terms. 'Diagnosis' and 'treatment' seem to suggest that the difficulties concerned are best investigated and dealt with under a medical rubric, and perhaps even that the cause of the problem is fundamentally a medical one. Most teachers will be familiar with the critique of this medical model (see Roe, 1978; Quicke, 1975), even if they might not think of it explicitly in these terms. They will know that hanging a medical label like dyslexia or phobia round a child's neck is at best a heavy-handed way to draw attention to a problem, and at worst can actually damage the child's chances of improvement by establishing a 'sick' identity from which it is difficult for him or her to escape and which has more negative that positive consequences. Rather than drawing attention to the difficulty in this way, they will know that the best approach is the low-key one that does not highlight the failure to the exclusion of all the positive attributes of the child concerned, but which nevertheless does not minimise the problem of handling what is usually a delicate situation at home and school. In a sense they are carrying out a 'diagnosis' by finding out more about the nature of the difficulty, and whether the cause is primarily the home or school or a combination of both, and they will be carrying out 'treatment' when they decide to help the child in some way in the school setting. But the difference is that their approval is all part of the way they normally organise their teaching — catering for individual need, fostering sociality between pupils and encouraging parental involvement.

The books discussed in this chapter have central characters who could be described as having emotional and/or learning difficulties in the Warnock sense. I have chosen them because each in its own way has something to say about how we perceive and deal with such difficulties.

The Honour of Being Dyslexic

Kerry, in T. Kennemore's *Wall of Words*, is approaching nine years of age, but cannot read even though she seems quite bright. She has to go to school, but is often sick either at home or at school. She goes to see various psychological and medical specialists, but resists all kinds of tests, and a diagnosis of her condition is never carried out to anyone's satisfaction, although according to Kim, her thirteen-year-old sister and narrator of the story, 'the experts gave their diagnosis: a clear case of school phobia' (p. 24).

This certainly appears to be the theory that the psychologist has at the back of his mind when he questions Kim about Kerry. He suggests that Kerry's problems may have something to do with the upset caused in the family by Dad leaving home. As Mrs Tate, Kerry's mother, puts it when discussing Kerry with Kim — 'He reckons that since her father went away Kerry's got a morbid fear that everyone's going to desert her. She's afraid that if she's at school all day everyone else — particularly me — may disappear while she's gone' (p. 72).

Such an explanation would me familiar to anyone who has read the psychiatric literature on school phobia (see, for example, Kahn and Nursten, 1968), where the usual interpretation preferred is that it is not a fear of school that is involved so much as an anxiety about being separated from mother, which is the main, underlying cause. This has been brought on by the mother's own anxiety and insecurity, in this instance precipitated by her husband leaving home. Such explanations have not been popular with some professionals, mainly because they tend to attract attention away from a combination of features in the school situation that may be responsible for or at least may be making a significant contribution to the problem. It is probably true that a psychologist, particularly an educational one, would tend to favour the separation-anxiety explanation less often than, say, a psychiatrist would, and so the psychologist here is certainly not typical (see Quicke, 1982, Ch. 2).

The conversation between Kim and the psychologist is interesting for the insight it gives into what it feels like to be on the receiving end of an expert trying to probe into matters which have, up until then, been very personal and private. Mr Gilbert keeps making suggestions in the form of not so subtle, 'see through' questions which makes Kim very uncomfortable, particularly when she realises that he is getting it all wrong. Even when she provides a fact which is counter to his hypothesis he still persists (as a good scientist would!) in attempting to obtain supporting evidence — a defensible strategy from his viewpoint, but it annoys Kim. She rebuffs his questions — 'I told you that', she exclaims with annoyance.

All his questions — about father going away, about Kim changing school, about the effect on mother, about the possibility of jealousy between Kerry and her younger sister Anna — seem to point the way to a diagnosis where family conflict plays a central role, but Kerry knows that this line of reasoning is false. She provides instance after instance where Gilbert's theories do not fit the facts, and the conversation goes round in circles. Kim is resentful — 'all her instincts were to hate him'. She wonders about the file he opens — 'Had it got private things written down about her mother and father? She wanted to snatch it out of his hands. She wanted to hit him' (p. 69).

As an example of a bad interview technique, this is well observed. The psychologist is not 'client centred' enough (see Rogers, 1951), he has a pet theory and seems to be sticking to it and thus reveals the danger of the traditional expert-approach to psychological problems, although this particular form of expert game is probably not typical of most psychologists (see Quicke, 1984).

All this is leading up to Kim's discovery of the 'true' diagnosis — that she is dyslexic — which is revealed to her by Mrs Hanharan, a teacher at Kim's school and a dyslexic herself. All the pieces of the puzzle fit in to place. The fact that Kim's uncle Jack and great grandmother couldn't read until late seems to suggest that there is a genetic component, which according to Mrs Hanharan is what one might expect if the problem is dyslexia. She goes on to explain that despite reading, writing and spelling difficulties, dyslexics are usually intelligent in other ways, that they often suffer from poor co-ordination, reversal tendencies, left-right confusion and poor verbal memory; that, like Kerry, they develop a memory for the spoken word to compensate for their poor visual memory (see Leach and Raybould, 1977, p. 6); and that there are different sorts of dyslexia and not everyone shows the same symptoms (p. 14).

A great weight is lifted from Kim's shoulders by this revelation and when Mrs Hanharan explains it to Kerry it makes an enormous impression — 'It's almost as if she thinks it's an honour to be dyslexic, if Mrs Hanharan is.'

The problem with this from a labelling viewpoint is that one label — 'dyslexia' — is used to 'save' the child from another label — 'retarded'. The psychological dynamic which Mrs Hanharan understands is Kerry's fear of being retarded or backward 'When she understands that she's in no way backward — that dyslexia is quite common, actually — I'm sure she'll be willing to work like mad to make up for all she's lost.' (p. 150).

Kerry, presumably, is sufficiently aware to understand what it means to suffer the fate of being called 'retarded' — a stigmatising label. This solves her problem, but from our viewpoint it still leaves many children labelled retarded who cannot join the dyslexics because they do not have the correct symptoms. For instance, the child who is below average on intelligence tests but who cannot read would not normally be called dyslexic, but may still have as serious a problem. There is no critique in the text of Mrs Hanharan's reliance on the notion of 'backward', because once you play the labels games, presumably using labels is all right as long as you use them correctly. But it is certainly not an 'honour' to be retarded or backwards. Even though in this instance the label seems to have helped Kerry, it is a dangerous game to use such exclusive categories. The diagnosis in any case is only partial. It does not explain why she had such a fear of being 'retarded', why this was so significant. Perhaps it was because two of her other sisters did so well at school. Kim, it transpires, was tested at six and found to be gifted. Anna is attractive, highly verbal and extrovert, and is offered a job as co-presenter of a children's radio programme. So when the psychologist suggests that the problem may have something to do with Kerry's sisters he certainly has a point, even though his reference to jealous, attention-seeking behaviour and separation anxiety may be an exaggeration.

In short, given the information that is provided in the book, it is not a clear-cut case of dyslexia. There are other contributing factors which are not emphasised but which are there in the text. The author falls into the same trap as many a bad professional diagnostician by not taking into account the total picture, and by homing in on a quasi-medical term to explain away the problem. With the diagnosis all sewn up and the patient pronounced a dyslexic, Kerry's character no longer interests us.

The book has other problems. Much of the text is not about Kerry or the 'wall of words'. We do not hear much from Kerry herself, or anything about her for long periods. It is all a bit fragmented, chopped into great chunks about each character, the only cohesion being provided by a hackneyed family-saga format. Another label utilised by the author is 'giftedness', which is applied to Kim. This relates to the sub-plot, which involves Kim learning something about her father and the nature of intelligence and education as well. Her father is also gifted, and Kim is impressed initially by his literary activity until she is enlightened by her mother, who reveals to her father's true nature — intelligent, yes, but one-dimensional, abstract and too academic, incapable of finishing any book he starts and basically a waster. This is why Mrs Tate does not want Kim to go to a school for gifted children.

She feels she would not obtain a good all-round education. Kim agrees that she would not like to go to a 'clever-clever' school. This relevation about father being useless despite his brains is one of the books more interesting insights, but it is a pity it has to remain unexplored. We would really have liked to have observed father throughout the book in more than one chapter, and to have made our own judgements rather than have mother provide us with the definitive explanation. We would also have appreciated hearing his side of the story.

In general, although some of the characters speak out against the expertism of psychologists and psychiatrists, there is an implied acceptance of the validity of the old-fashioned medical-expert approach with its labels and explanations. The author takes on the role of a psychiatrist through his characters, makes them use jargon like 'dyslexia' and 'giftedness', makes them search for causes and provide instant diagnoses. IQs are treated as 'facts' like dyslexia. But does this jargon help to illuminate character and relationships? It seems merely to substitute the stereotypes of experts for those of lay people.

Seeing Yourself as the Experts See You

A similar point might be made about L. Mildiner's and B. House's *The Gates*, which employs the medical category of 'school phobia' portrayed as an illness which the two working-class heroes have. The story, however, is not about the search for a cause so much as what happens when such a cause is diagnosed. It is a tale of two youngsters who have an uncontrollable fear of school. In the introduction we learn that it was written by young authors who themselves had this problem, and was based upon 'true life incidents, upon things that have happened to us.' The two central characters are Geoff Moller and David Cook, both of whom find it impossible to adapt to the comprehensive school and truant so regularly that they are placed in a tutorial class, and eventually are both sent to a day school for maladjusted pupils.

Geoff experiences dizzy spells connected with the thought of going to secondary school. His problems began when he had to leave the 'shell' of his primary school — 'he had to stay at home to be safe inside the shell which was to take the place of Stanford Primary School.' He is described as having 'agoraphobia — so he was terrified to slip out of the house for fear he would stop breathing and die' (p. 12). He is referred to a psychiatrist, who suggests that he attends a tutorial class, which he successfully manages to do after some initial reluctance.

David's development is portrayed in a similar way. He cannot bear the thought of another day of being bullied, pushed and shoved on the crowded stairs of a 'massive comprehensive with one thousand, nine hundred boys, to David, all seven feet tall' (p. 18). And so he also runs off, and that is the beginning of regular truanting. Every day the 'illogical' side of him gets the upper hand, and he runs out of school at the slightest opportunity. He is also sent to a psychiatrist, who tells him that he is suffering from 'school phobia', and after a number of placements in other schools he is also persuaded to attend the tutorial class.

The boys make a successful adjustment to their new classes and to the maladjusted school they are sent to. They have a favourable attitide to both their special placements despite being apprehensive at first particularly about the maladjusted school. They think that the teachers are more sympathetic and understanding and have time to talk to the pupils and develop relationships with them. The timetable is more flexible, and the curriculum is informal and more interesting. Acceptance and a problem-solving approach rather than moral condemnation is the orientation of the teacher.

At this point it is worth noting that this novel is essentially autobiographical, and up to a point one would agree with Worpole (1975) that it gains artistic wholeness 'with a device that no adult writer would see: that having gone through the many experiences in the book the two boys decide to transform their knowledge.' We therefore should not judge it by adult standards of what constitutes a well-written novel. There is an appeal to authenticity, to the honesty of the expression of genuine experience, 'uncompromised by the appeal to stereotyped situations that occurs so frequently in the commercially published 'concerned' adolescent fiction' (p. 82).

It is true that these boys do not employ the psychiatrically influenced stereotype of the school phobic as having problems more rooted in the home rather than the school. It is the school which produces fear in them — teachers with no time for you, a boring curriculum, authoritarian teachers, no space for personal development, massive buildings and too many other children, some of them brutalised by the system. As Leila Berg remarks on the back cover of *The Gates*: 'what comes over most is the bull-headed insanity of the compulsory school system.'

Another refreshing aspect is the description of the boys' adventures

– sexual and otherwise – which it is difficult to imagine an adult writing about without dramatising or twisting into something 'more interesting'. They are matter-of-fact accounts and contain some fascinating detail. The brushes with authority outside school have a humorous edge, but nevertheless we can understand how insulting policemen and bus conductors can be to lads like them. For example, a policeman stops them for no reason other than that he suspects that they have stolen the bikes they are riding, and starts asking them ludicrous questions like 'What make are your brakes?' – which makes the boys feel angry because they do not like being talked to in that manner. At the end of this episode they are locked up for a short time in a 'cold, empty room' at the police station.

The authenticity of the book lies in the telling details contained in descriptions of such encounters. In another incident a bus conductor rubs them up the wrong way by spotting that they should have paid an extra two pence bus fare. These are the experiences of youth in our law and order society which adults are rarely in a position to share, and the book is worth reading on account of these episodes alone.

But this writer has misgivings about the book as a whole. These boys are clearly reasonably happy with their placements in a special unit and then a special school. There is no resentment or feeling of stigmatisation expressed. Both establishments function as 'havens' for them and they seem to get a lot from them. The relationship between the boys grows. We see them sharing fears together at a fairground, 'having a laugh' and 'chatting up birds', playing in the football team, and having sexual adventures. They eventually develop a loyalty to the school and what it stands for. They strongly object to a girl who asks them if they go to the 'mental school round the corner'. They appreciate the way the teachers treat them. They start to understand that other kids in the school have similar problems to them. They become less 'agoraphobic'.

However, despite all of this we are left with the suspicion that the 'good' adults, like the psychiatrists and teachers who see them as having a problem, may paradoxically be more intrusive than the 'bad' adults like bus conductors, supermarket owners and policemen. The boys seem to accept the psychiatric definition of themselves as having a 'phobia', but why is it necessary for them to have this 'sick' label? Their fears are often described as irrational – one of the boys, indeed, refers to the 'illogical' side of him getting the upper hand. But these fears are not phobias in the clinical sense. They are perfectly rational and stem from their dislike of a dehumanising school system, as the boys themselves suggest. Giving the boys a psychiatric identity leads to a quasi-medical treatment. The boys go to special establishments to be 'treated' – an essential ingredient of which are chats with a psychotherapist.

There is confusion here because we are not sure what weight to give school in comparison with other factors as the cause of their 'sickness'. The boys seem to be special cases, but we are not told what is so different about them that distinguishes them from other pupils who have adverse reactions to school. Paradoxically, we do not understand the nature of these two boys' aversion precisely because the psychiatric term 'phobia' is introduced as a gloss on that experience. It is clearly not enough to know that school is too boring and teachers unsympathetic. That is part of the story; it applies to the majority of truants as well as to this particular form of truancy. The medical term seems to get in the way of these boys providing a more detailed account of their particular experiences which would give a fuller picture of their psychological development. In fact, we can see how this imposition of a medical term has even boxed them off from their own experiences. It does nothing to illuminate their psychology – for themselves or for the reader.

The worrying thing is that they eventually seem to accept that certain behaviours are typical of boys with their sort of problem, as if being labelled perhaps legitimised certain behaviour like temper tantrums, which previously they would not have wished to associate with themselves. Towards the end there is one very revealing passage:

It was Christmas. The season of goodwill to all men. It was the time of year when people who usually went around attacking other people, or stealing things, start being good, kind, generous and loving. Well, for one day at least.

Sheila was one of those people. A few weeks earlier she had thrown a fire extinguisher through a window after losing her temper. Geoff and David had got used to her tantrums. At first it was a bit frightening, but now it didn't worry them so much, as most of the children in Selton had violent tempers. Even Geoff and David . . . But then it was a school for children with problems and nearly always part of the problem was a violent temper. (p. 118).

Now clearly Geoff had this problem. It had got him into trouble before, but was it also David's problem? David managed to attend judo classes without any difficulty and behaved in a controlled manner there. Is it possible, one wonders, that he was beginning to imitate the behaviour of the other boys at Selton?

There are a number of other confusing aspects. Geoff is described as agoraphobic and yet spends his lunch hours walking round the local market asking stall holders if they need any help, and eventually obtains a part-time job in a supermarket. In fact, neither of the boys seem to warrant the label 'agoraphobic' which is a more appropriate term for the pathological state that adults sometimes find themselves in rather than for a developmental problem of adolescence.

These books, *Wall of Words* and *The Gates*, though vastly different in style and structure, share a commitment to a psycho-medical description of a problem, the consequences of which are not explored by the characters and which results in an uncritical acceptance by children of a term imposed on them by an expert. This is another example of a counterproductive treatment of special needs. It seems to be part of each author's intention to illuminate the nature of and thereby de-stigmatise certain educational and psychological problems, but this is done by using explanations of experience of a type which limits the literary exploration of these problems. The authors on the one hand seem sensitive to the labelling issue, but on the other resolve the characters' problems in ways which could ultimately have precisely the opposite effect to that intended.

In the case of *The Gates* we also have what amounts to a justification for an institution called a maladjusted school, despite the well-known criticism that such schools are not the answer to maladjustment (see Galloway and Goodwin, 1979, pp. 40-1). They direct attention away from a consideration of how normal schools can be changed so that children like this will not be afraid to attend. If a novel is to have contemporary relevance it surely must have something to say about the integration issue and question the role of the special school? It is a major weakness of *The Gates* that it does not do this.

We Shall Not Be Typed

A book which deals with problem behaviour and the labelling issue in a way which does not involve succumbing to the heavy-handed embrace of psycho-medical terminology is Gene Kemp's *The Turbulent Term of Tyke Tiler*. This is a fast-moving story, written in a lively style and full of humour and surprises for the reader. The main surprise is that Tyke, whom most readers assume to be a boy, turns out to be a girl. There are in fact plenty of clues in the text as to her true sex, but it is revealing of one's own stereotypal thinking that these tend to be ignored on the first reading. Tyke (or Theodora) is no old-fashioned tomboy caricature. She is an active, assertive, confident, jokey, high-spirited twelve-year-old who clearly does not like to be called Theodora, because it just does not suit her, not because she has a subconscious longing to be a boy. Her anger at being called Theodora by a teacher she particularly dislikes (Mrs Somers) stems from her resistance to an adult imposing an identity on her, trying to make her someone she does not want to be.

It is this suspicion of adult typing which is the key to understanding her relationship with Danny, a boy of limited ability and with a speech defect, whom she befriends. She clearly sees it as an adult imposition that Danny should be categorised in a way that would lead to his being segregated from others. For her, Danny has problems, but there is more to him than that. She is genuinely happy to 'knock about' with him and do things with him both in and out of school. She is no do-gooder, and certainly not unrealistic in her perception of him. She recognises his limitations, but sees other facets which taken together make up a personality which she can relate to. And Danny is no passive defective. He may not be all that bright, but he is active enough and keeps her on her toes! Even though he is, in her own words, as 'thick as two planks', he can generally get her to do the things he wants.

Tyke certainly does not mince her words when talking to or talking about Danny, 'You idiotic imbecile', she shouts at him on one occasion. But she is using these words in a jokey way. She knows that the relationship is strong enough for Danny to take it from her. What really upsets her is other people treating Danny as if he was nothing but a certain type of child — people who would not call him an 'idiotic imbecile' or 'as thick as two planks', but would dehumanise him with their own seemingly neutral terminology. When she overhears a discussion between teachers about whether or not Danny should go to a special school instead of the comprehensive, and hears Mrs Somers referring to this school as being able to deal with children of that type, she wants to cry out 'that Danny Price, my friend, was not a child of that type, that he was funny and nice and all right and that I could tell what he said perfectly clearly' (p. 73). She resents Danny being typed, just as she resents people, particularly the Mrs Somers of this world, attempting to type her.

In order to make sure that Danny is not sent to a special school, she decides to put into effect an emergency plan of a deviant nature. She steals the Verbal Reasoning Test which the top year is about to take, and coaches Danny on it. To everyone's surprise he does well enough to go to the comprehensive school. The plan almost backfires because she herself does so well that there is talk of her going to a school for the gifted. Luckily such schools are against her father's principles, and she is unlikely to be forced into attending one.

Tyke's socialist family background has obviously got something to do with her lack of snobbishness and her positive attitude towards Danny, but there is no doubt the teachers also play an important role in recognising and in a sense validating the growing friendship between them. Not all the teachers are so facilitating. As Tyke informs us on page 47 'We're arranged in groups and I'm allowed to sit by Danny so as I can help him. Mrs Somers didn't let me, last year, but Sir does.'

The 'Sir' referred to here is Mr Merchant, whose attitude reflects his progressive approach and is in marked contrast to that of the rigid and authoritarian Mrs Somers. It is precisely because of his progressive philosophy that Mr Merchant can see the need to allow Tyke to help Danny. In a sense what the author beautifully demonstrates here is that in a school where this philosophy is dominant the integration of children with special needs almost takes care of itself. Given that the ethos of the school promotes relationships between girls like Tyke and boys like Danny, what possible reason could there be for suggesting that Danny's needs would best be met in a special school? This story, then, represents among other things a very powerful statement for the policy of integration. It is convincing because the author allows us to see the genuineness of the friendship between them, and we do not feel that Danny is being patronised by Tyke or that Tyke is in some way losing out because of time spent with Danny. We feel as angry as Tyke that Danny is referred to as a 'type' suitable for a special school.

Is Catharsis Enough?

Another book where the role of the school is explored in an interesting way is Linda Hoy's *Your Friend, Rebecca*. Again, the problems of the adolescent heroine are described without recourse to psycho-medical terminology, and she is not treated as a case of school phobia or any other kind of case. Yet we obtain a fuller picture of the nature of her disturbance and poor adjustment to school than we do of the characters in either the *Wall of Words* or *The Gates*. Rebecca is clearly a depressed adolescent who feels rejected by the world since her mother died, and has never really come to terms with life without mother. She hates school and most of her teachers, but even at the start of the novel has some recognition of her own contribution to her own problems. She admits that she is 'a bit of a mess'. When mum was alive everything was warm and cosy at home. Now she has to come home to a cold house and cook (if cook is the right term for her pathetic efforts) her own dinner as well as her father's. The relationship with father is the key one in the story. They do not communicate with each other and she thinks that it is better this way. Life at home is depressing. She goes to her room to escape father, but she cannot settle down to doing much homework. For the rest of the evening she sits in front of the television watching programmes which bore her.

Many of the unpleasant or boorish features of school which even in normal times would irritate her arouse strong feelings of hatred in her current state. She gets into trouble with the teachers, some of whom treat her in the same insensitive way as they do children who do not have her problems. It is the familiar approach which perhaps most children just accept as 'school, bloody school', but it exasperates her to such a degree that on one occasion she loses control. She is accused of insolence by the headmistress, Miss Hoggitt, whom she has nicknamed 'The Hog'. She feels the interrogation has Gestapo-like features. The questions are as predictable as her responses in this game of 'dressing down', which teachers do daily to children (see Rosser and Harré, 1976). Each knows the role she is supposed to play and the responses that are expected as the ritual proceeds.

'What do you want to do when you leave school?' she asks me. She even makes that sound threatening.

But I know about that one. I'm supposed to say a posh job like Prime Minister or a crematorium assistant, then she'll tell me all the qualifications you need and how hard you've got to work for them . . .

Rebecca, however, is in a mood to play the game up to a point.

I'm not bothered. I say I don't know.
'Well that's just typical, isn't it? Rebecca.'
I'm not supposed to answer that. I just have to look ashamed. It's quite easy. I just wish it were over with though. (p. 30).

Later there is an interesting example of the way such a ritual can suddenly become oppressive for the adolescent with a problem and can bring out what appears to be 'disturbed' behaviour. The Hog is going on about 'women who stay at home', who cook and wash up and polish the furniture, and expresses her opinion that 'that's all there is to their lives, Rebecca.' A routine enough statement from a career-minded teacher which girl pupils no doubt are used to hearing, but in this instance Rebecca is needled. It seems to her that the home-making role of a mother is precisely what she and her father are missing most, and it angers her to hear The Hog delivering what amounts to an attack on her mother. She eventually explodes, forgetting the teacher–pupil game, and behaves in a way which is definitely out of order. 'I hate you . . . just bloody-well leave me alone' she says as she walks out and slams the door.

The language here is extreme, reflecting the hatred she feels – 'I could kill her'. The power in her voice frightens her. Her hatred for the teacher is matched only by that which she feels for her father. A psychological low-point is reached when, realising that she has gone over the top at school, she decides to butter father up by making him a special tea and then, when he is in a good mood, to persuade him to intervene on her behalf at school. But her plans are dashed when he arrives home late. Moreover, she later discovers that he has stolen money from her moneybox with which to go drinking. The final straw is when he comes home drunk and she hears him vomiting in the garden – 'That's the kind of father I've got.' (p. 46).

From this point on we see her gradually begin to come to terms with the emotions which frighten her. One of the few subjects at school which appeals to her is drama. In drama she can act out her feelings about school and her father without fear of reprisals. The play they are doing is *King Lear*, which has themes which are pertinent to her current emotional state. The pupils do not read from a script but improvise around the plot, and this seems to work for her. Catharsis takes place. The father-surrogate is a boy called Darren whom she fancies, but he too like her father has let her down and is the object of her hatred. He plays the part of Lear and she Regan, and she lets him have it with full power and venom. After which, with Darren standing there 'speechless and open-mouthed', she ceases to shake, and having released her anger feels calm and composed.

Drama lessons also involve group discussion of emotional topics. It is in one of these sessions when they are discussing 'rejection' that she realises how meaningful this topic is for her. She is clearly beginning to understand her condition.

> Everybody knows what it means. They've all got plenty to say about it anyway. But, as I sit cross-legged on the floor and listen to them all chattering away, it seems as though I'm the only one who really understands what rejection is all about. (p. 88)

Yet she is still fragile and very easily plunged back into darkness. In one scene, which she plays with the teacher in a one-to-one encounter, she seems to regress. 'I pull up my knees so I'm curled up like a baby racoon in a nest and rock myself gently backwards and forwards, moaning softly. Rocking my baby and rocking myself, moaning and whimpering.' (p. 90).

Drama, however, is not the only activity which helps her come to terms with her emotions. She also finds peace in the quieter atmosphere of Quaker meetings where really 'good ideas suddenly spring from nowhere inside your head', and which acts as a complement to the hectic drama sessions by providing a space where she can reflect more soberly on her situation.

Eventually, she begins to take more of an interest in her school work. She is at peace enough with herself to settle down and write a funny story for English homework about King Kong trying to get through customs. Of more significance, however, is her gradually changing perception of her father. She becomes less egocentric and begins to see things from his point of view. When she finds him crying, she realises that he has been suffering too. She recalls lines from *King Lear* − 'the oldest hath borne most' and 'speak what we feel'. She realises that she has been so preoccupied with her own feelings that she had never thought about how sad he must have been. She finds the strength to reach out to him

> I look down at his reflection in the mirror and smile weakly. For a moment or two our eyes meet and then he smiles at me gently. We don't say anything but I feel a kind of satisfaction. As if I've taken a step forward. (p. 140)

An interesting point here is that Rebecca achieves her step forward, she gets through this worst period of her life 'when I got really low and depressed', without the help of the experts such as psychologists, psychiatrists, social workers or psychotherapists. There are enough positive features in her social environment − the drama teacher and the Quakers – to pull her through. Different teachers in the school make different contributions – some exacerbate her condition, others help her. To what extent are the teachers aware of what is happening to Rebecca? They certainly know of her problems. Miss Hoggitt is aware that her mother has died, and Miss Gloucester the drama teacher says on one occasion that she knows it has been 'difficult at home for you these last twelve months' (p. 109). We must assume that Miss Gloucester does have some understanding of the role of drama in Rebecca's emotional development, but there is not much evidence of a planned campaign to help Rebecca via drama.

Miss Gloucester clearly operates according to her own model of the relationship between drama and personality development, yet she is not portrayed as an expert in the sense that the term has been used in this chapter. Neither she nor any other adult 'explains away' Rebecca's condition or stamps her with a psycho-medical label like 'maladjusted' or 'clinically depressed'. Rebecca is not being 'treated' by psycho-dramatic therapy, but is being educated emotionally in the normal school context in a normal lesson. She is not singled out as a special case, but achieves her readjustment in an integrated setting.

However, it seems to me that there is a question about the way this emotional education is portrayed in the story – a question we can ask without implying that the best thing for Rebecca would have been a referral to the child guidance clinic. Nor am I assuming that teachers need extra special training from, say, a qualified psychotherapist before they can handle emotional problems; that is, training over and above normal teacher training both initial and in-service. Giving children individual attention and support in times of crisis is what sensitive human beings do, trained or untrained. But in this novel the teacher, although obviously aware of catharsis and the emotional impact of drama, seems to adopt an approach which does strike one as dubious. In the dramatic encounter she is quite ruthless and does not pull any punches. The situation to be acted out involves a girl who has left her husband, but whose sister refuses to put her up.

I'm getting soaked to the skin here in the thunderstorm and the baby's writhing about now, screaming, I can hardly hold it . . . 'I'm your sister!' I shout at her. 'Your own flesh and blood.'

'So what?' she snarls. The stuck-up bitch. 'I've got me own family to look after an' so 'ave you. Now, get off 'ome.' (p. 90)

All this is fair enough. The exchange does have an effect on Rebecca.

It produces the regression referred to above. The passage quoted continues

> My eyes are closed . . . there's no one in the world that loves me . . . there's nobody to care about me . . . the well of loneliness starts to creep back through the air holes in my mind . . . I think I want to die. (pp. 90-1)

On that note, however, the chapter ends. Are we to assume that this has been a successful lesson? Up to a point, but it is worrying that there is no suggestion that the teacher needs to do anything else. Having reduced Rebecca to a state where she feels that she wants to die, the lesson presumably ends, and Rebecca is left having to cope by herself with the feelings released. This is surely a bad way to go about helping someone with an emotional problem? At the very least, the teacher should have had a quiet chat with her when the other children had gone. Instead, there is no one, apparently, apart from Rebecca herself, to pick up the pieces. This is a thoughtless omission on the teacher's part, but the reader is confused because Miss Gloucester is clearly being portrayed as a caring teacher. The author does not unveil Miss Gloucester's intentions, but we suspect that she approves of her as a teacher. Rebecca certainly does. But she is a teacher who seems to be playing a risky game, with too little concern for the consequences. Perhaps underpinning all this is some half-baked theory of the author that catharsis is enough.

Nevertheless, this book has many strengths, and raises a number of issues about the treatment of so-called 'maladjusted' behaviour. It also provides a convincing portrait of a girl with a temporary emotional disturbance. We can fully understand how her behaviour at school is largely a reflection of what is happening at home and how important it is for the teacher to be aware of this. Yet, at the same time it is crucial that teachers should understand that what they do in school can make a contribution to the solution of a problem which is not primarily school based. In recent times, many teachers have begun to accept that the reverse is also true. Parents can often help to resolve an educational problem. There is, in fact, a growing interest in the role that parents and other adults can play in relation to activities, like the teaching of reading, for example, which would previously have been considered the sole preserve of the teacher.

A Right and a Wrong Way to Teach

A book which is relevant to the issue of parental involvement in teaching is S. Haigh's *Watch For The Ghost*. This is a fairly run-of-the-mill story relying on the usual interest hooks of school ghosts, dogs and parents who do not understand, but it is well written and has one or two interesting features. Dan is in the last year at junior school and has not yet learned to read, partly on account of his having missed a lot of schooling in the infants through illness. The teachers have been too busy to give him the extra help he needs, and he has dropped further and further behind. His teacher, Mr Oakes, does not handle the situation very well. 'What are you doing? Daydreaming again? . . . You'll never learn to read if you spend your time daydreaming', he says to him in front of the class, who watch gleefully as Dan receives yet another dressing-down from the teacher.

Two approaches to teaching Dan to read are described, both of which involve adults other than teachers. They make an interesting contrast in that one is successful and the other is an example of how not to do it. The latter involves Dan's parents. The parents row about his backwardness, and mother is persuaded of the necessity of a visit to school to find out what is wrong. We do not know what was said by the school, but the upshot is that father decides to help him with his reading and takes him to a bookshop to buy a book. The first mistake father makes is to purchase a 'babyish looking book with a duck on the front'. Dan wonders how long the teaching at home is going to last before dad loses his temper. He does not have long to wait. There is an initial improvement, but his relations with dad deteriorate after an incident involving his sister and we are back to square one. The interaction between father and son that follows should make anyone who sees parental involvement as a cure-all for reading problems think again.

'You don't deserve to have this extra help', he said. 'Now come on. We are going to start page three.'

Dan found himself staring at page three; he managed the first two words and then stuck at the third. He'd seen the word before but he couldn't think what it was. There were so many words! Mr Rivers sat fidgeting in annoyance.

'Come on', he said, 'you know that word'.

Anxiously Dan made a wild guess. 'This', he said, looking enquiringly at his father.

Mr Rivers' eyes were bulging and his cheeks red. He stabbed at the word with an angry finger.

'You had this word on page one!' he shouted 'You managed it then!' He turned back to page one and pointed fiercely at the same word.

'What's that?' he demanded. Dan froze. For some reason he just could not remember. 'I don't know', he mumbled. He seized the book and flung it down violently.

'He just can't be bothered!' he shouted at Mrs Rivers. 'Wretched boy! He's just plain stupid and lazy. He'll end up in a mental home. There I go spending time and money to help him to read and he can't even learn a little word like that. I'm going to the pub.' (p. 104)

Clearly, the message here is that parents should not be encouraged to help their children with reading if there is a likelihood of this sort of emotionally charged interchange occurring. Father's involvement is totally counterproductive. As adults, we can have a certain sympathy for him because he, like the teachers in school, is obviously pressed for time. The family are not well off, and mother has to work overtime to make ends meet. She is also the sort of mother who worries too much about what the neighbours think. However, by the end of the book they have stopped 'quarrelling about how he was going to get on in the big school'. Their attitude has improved mainly because Dan has been helped in his reading by another character whose methods are exemplary.

This character is Granny Venn, whom Dan first saw as 'the face at the window' and thought was a ghost. She is the only person who seems to have time for him. He first meets her when he is invited to tea at the Venns' house after an incident involving the theft of their dog. The police are involved, but Dan has just been carried away by his own childish designs and all thought that his taking the dog was stealing did not enter his head. Dan is fascinated by the 'hair raising' stories in Granny Venn's big book, which she reads to him. He comes back for more and again and again, and each time he not only listens to the story but watches the words carefully as she reads them. He soon manages to follow her 'reading with his eyes'. Then, at last he begins to feel confident enough to have a go himself.

'One day', he said, 'I think I could read some of that Gran'. She handed him the book.

'Have a go then', she said, 'and if you don't know the words, never mind. I'll tell you the ones you don't know'.

It was harder than he'd thought, but Gran sat calmly telling him words the minute he hesitated.

'Well done', she exclaimed when he'd read a page. So every time after that, he would try to read a page, and Gran would sit patiently, making encouraging comments and helping him whenever he got stuck. She never seemed to mind how bad he was and Dan felt he would do anything to please her. He began to practise reading in secret, so that he could surprise her.

At school his work improved and he was summoned to Mrs Fisher for a gold star. (p. 118)

Prior to this his relationship with Mrs Fisher had not been good, and her attitude had been an important factor contributing to his difficulty. His stock with her reached an all-time low after the stealing of the dog incident. Dan's reactions to this teacher are well observed by the author. Like Tyke Tiler in the *Turbulent Term* and Rebecca in *Your Friend, Rebecca*, his relationship with a teacher constantly involves a determined effort not to allow the teacher to get the upper hand, particularly in relation to her efforts to persuade him to see himself as she sees him, in other words, to define the child's identity against the child's will. Children are always in a weak position because their lack of experience makes prediction of teacher behaviour difficult, and they are always being caught off guard.

Dan was uncertain about how Mrs Fisher was going to react to the stealing incident — 'he thought perhaps Mrs Fisher would understand', but in the event she is not at all sympathetic. She lets him know what she thinks of him, and he has difficulty in warding off the negative self-image which she seems to be stamping in to him: 'He couldn't fight against it. He couldn't take what she was saying. Surely, he wasn't as bad as she made out? Cruel, selfish, inconsiderate, dishonest! Surely, he wasn't all those things and bad at school work too?' (p. 40).

The only resource he has to keep him alive as a person in his own right is hatred — 'I hate her, I hate them all'. He sobs one sob of rage, not sorrow. The next time he is in receipt of a lecture from Mrs Fisher we see a development. 'This time he did not cry. It was as though a hard shell had grown up around him, protecting him, gathering another layer for every telling-off he had' (p. 103).

Thanks mainly to Granny Venn the layers are gradually peeled off.

Summary

In this chapter I have discussed books where one of the central characters might be described as having a learning or emotional difficulty. Such difficulties are often conceptualised in terms which presuppose the acceptance of a medical-model approach. Where this is the case, my argument is that such terminology makes a negative contribution to the literary exploration of themes and issues revealed in the characters and their interactions.

Thus, in Kennemore's *Wall of Words*, despite the interesting critique of the expert role in certain parts of the book, we are asked to look upon Kerry's difficulties as explicated by the 'fact' of her being 'dyslexic'. This has the effect of ruling out ambiguity and uncertainty in relation to Kerry's psychology. (The term is also used in a way which reinforces the stigma associated with other terms like 'backward' or 'retarded'.) A similar point can be made about the medical term 'school phobia' employed in Mildiner's and House's *The Gates*. Using such a term seems to reduce and circumscribe rather than enhance the boys' descriptions of their own experiences.

In Kemp's *The Turbulent Term of Tyke Tiler* there is a resistance to construing difficulties in medical or other expert terminology which is part and parcel of the heroine's objection to herself and her friend being stereotyped by adults. Likewise, in Hoy's *Your Friend, Rebecca* the heroine's emotional problems are explained without recourse to the jargon of experts. Both these books contain vivid accounts of the interaction between children with problems and their teachers, and demonstrate the role of the school in the creation, perpetuation and resolution of difficulties. Haigh's *Watch For The Ghost* (altogether a simpler book written for a younger age group) also contains insights into educational processes both inside but particularly outside school. Again, the author avoids employing medical terms to categorise the hero's reading difficulties.

TO LOVE AND BE LOVED

Conventional novels on love between an adolescent boy and girl where one or both are disabled are often love stories in the worst sense of the term. They are superficial, romantic, sentimental, and reinforce cultural stereotypes of behaviour in a love relationship which are basically sexist (Nightingale, 1974). The girl is the one who is more dependent or who is preoccupied with having and holding on to a boyfriend. She can be beautiful and rich or just plain and ordinary, but in either case her character is subsumed under what amounts to an almost total obsession with the boy. The boy, on the other hand, is more active, takes more initiatives and has interests outside the relationship. If he has the disability then the girl becomes preoccupied with caring for him. He is often the handsome, intelligent and well-off hero struck down by a disability which he was not born with, and it is indeed a tragedy, but thanks to his girlfriend's devotion he wins through and all ends happily ever after. The concept of 'love' in such relationships does not usually have a clear meaning. It is something that they just fall into.

The Man Who Has Everything

The kind of book I have in mind here is Monica Edward's *A Wind is Blowing*. The hero is Meryon Fairbrass, a 'Man Who Has Everything' (p. 9). He has that romantic gipsy look, 'except for quite brilliant blue eyes, like those of a Siamese cat' (p. 8). He lives in a nice home in a beautiful coastal area, drives his own car and is very intelligent, judging from his excellent A-level grades. By his side is Tanzin – beautiful, intelligent and rides horses. Tragedy strikes, however, when he is blinded by the ammonia thrown at him by a bank robber whom, being the perfect citizen Meryon is, he has tried to apprehend in the street. This makes him bitter at first, but it is a noble sort of bitterness. He does not want to continue his relationship with Tanzin on the grounds that 'I won't be anybody's damaged article' (p. 29).

But the loyal Tanzin is not so easily put off. On the advice of her father, the vicar, she decides that the best course of action is for her to get to know as much as she can about the blind and also do something practical to help them. She writes to the Royal National Institute for the Blind and corresponds on tape with two blind boys who live in different parts of the country. Eventually, she re-establishes contact with Meryon by sending him some tapes and also a rejected sheepdog, which turns out to be the means of Meryon's re-entry into social life. Training this dog — Meg — to be a guide dog gives him a renewed interest in life, and also leads to his reunification with Tanzin, who assists him with this task. The rest of the story is a succession of happy outcomes as Meryon gradually becomes rehabilitated, culminating in the happiest event of all when he goes to Spain for an operation on his eyes which enables him to see again. Previously he had refused to consider a corneal graft on the grounds that being the stalwart, independent person he was he did not believe that he was as helpless as some of the others on the waiting list who should therefore have had the operation before him. However, he agrees to the operation when it so happens that a relative who has bequeathed her eyes to him is killed in an aircrash. When he returns to England, both he and Meg play a prominent role in capturing the bank robber who blinded him.

This is a safe novel with a formula plot. The blindness is only temporary, merely a hiccup in the beautiful lives of well-off and intelligent people. Tanzin herself is good, caring but uninteresting, and like all girls when the going gets rough at the end of the story she takes a back seat. She is, of course, devoted to Meryon, but what girl wouldn't be? He is a man who has everything — even A-levels — and like all heroes he gets the villain in the end, with the help of his faithful dog.

The Girl Who Had Enough Black in Her Life

In the rest of this chapter I want to discuss novels which do not stick to the conventional format and which are more challenging. Kata's *A Patch of Blue* is interesting from a number of viewpoints. The eighteen-year-old heroine Selina is the daughter of a prostitute, Roseann, and has been blinded accidently by her mother's throwing acid at her intended for her returning husband. She lives an unenviable existence in a downtown flat with a mother who rejects her, and a grandfather who loves her but goes out to drown his sorrows in drink every night.

The story is about how she establishes a loving relationship with a man considerably older than herself whom she meets regularly in the park and who cares for her in a way she has never known before. He helps to expand her horizons, teaches her things, and generally gives her hope. Thus, we have a male character who is for once caring and sensitive and a girl who is certainly not beautiful in a conventional sense – she was, in fact, disfigured by the acid as well as blinded. But the book has even more surprises. Gordon, Selina's new-found lover, turns out to be black, and although this is foreshadowed in the text (for instance, the precedence he gives to the notion of tolerance over friendship – 'without tolerance there can be no friendship' (p. 51)) it is still unexpected as far as she is concerned.

It is Selina's reaction to this knowledge about Gordon's racial identity which is the high point of the book. We can see tension welling up in her as she struggles to come to terms with the conflicting strands of her experience. This is no gentle, blind girl, all nice and pink and good, but a girl who has been brought up in brutalising circumstances which have interacted with her blindness to produce a peculiar kind of hatred. She tries to suppress this hatred, but it runs deep in her make up, as prejudice often does. She has for years hated everything black because that is all she has ever seen – 'I had enough black in my life' (p. 7) – and this has reinforced the hatred of 'niggers' instilled in her by the white adults in her life. And so her reaction is predictable. When she hears a white man shout at Gordon 'Leave her be. Leave Selina be – You goddam nigger', she is thrown off guard, becomes mixed up with thoughts and emotions flying this way and that, and instead of defending Gordon, comes out with – 'Get your hands off of me. You black, you goddam nigger' (p. 108).

But this is only a temporary 'madness', because thanks to Gordon she has been given a new strength to resist the brutal messages of her previous life and has been lifted out of the 'dark well'. She is full of remorse. She had been blinded emotionally and intellectually as well as physically by her upbringing – 'I wept for the blindness of my heart and mind; for my intolerance; and my meaningless, cheap hatred – hatred of a thing that didn't rate hatred.' (p. 171).

This is an excellent portrayal of the complex emotions of a blind, white girl brought up in a racist society, and like most of the better books of this genre manages to contextualise the disability in a way which not only tells us something about the experience of the disability, but also about the society in which it is located. The book ends with an attempt at a message of hope: 'A tiny ray of light lightened my darkness. The smallest beginning of could it be – hope – was born in my heart. Couldn't I, Selina, beat a drum, ring a clear-sounding bell for someone else – for something.' (p. 172).

Although she is worried at one point that she has destroyed her new self, she has in fact been re-born. But the reader may ask: What does Gordon get out of it all? As he is set upon by the racist mob who think he is attacking Selina, he cries out 'You are destroying me, Selina.' Selina thinks he is mistaken — 'He had been wrong! The strength, so part of him, would help him over this' (p. 170).

The reader, however, is not so sure. Gordon is still left with his 'problem'. She is indirectly going to help him by fighting prejudice in her own way, by ringing a clear-sounding bell. But will that be enough? When the crowd gathers round her after the incident, and after she hears the first soft beat of her drum, a voice says 'She's in a bad way, for sure.' (p. 172).

So what will it mean to white racists when she beats the drum for 'tolerance'? Won't she be regarded as in a state of shock, or in a bad way, still? Someone whose views, therefore, need not be taken seriously?

The Lady of Shalott

In *A Patch of Blue* we can understand why Selina and Gordon fall in love, but the actual development of this strong emotional bond between them is not described in the kind of detail one would like to fully understand what was happening between them. It is not enough to know that they met frequently and fell in love. What was the qualitative change which enabled them to talk about love? People experience love in different ways. The author cannot assume we all know what she means by the term.

A novel which is particularly insightful on the nature of love is Cordelia Jones's *The View From the Window*. This is also about an eighteen-year-old disabled girl who has a relationship with a much older man. The girl in question is Irene, who has rheumatoid arthritis, which necessitates her going into hospital for weeks on end for courses of treatment. She becomes fascinated with Ian Pollard, who is confined to a wheelchair after an accident but is not permanently invalided. He used to be a patient in the hospital but has moved to a cottage nearby. Like Selina in *A Patch of Blue*, she feels cut off from a normal life, and like the Lady of Shalott she is shut up in her island castle whence she watches the world go by. Yet, though vunerable and inexperienced, she has a good critical faculty which enables her to analyse her emotions and reflect on her relationships. At first, although she agrees with many of his opinions and admires the artificial aids he has invented for the disabled, herself included, there is something about him —

mainly his tendency to be arrogant — which annoys her. However, as she gets to know him better, she keeps finding that her previous assessments have been wrong, and he is much less short-sighted and self-opinionated than she imagined him to be at first. There are some interesting insights here into Irene's thought and emotional development. The reason she slightly dislikes him initially is that she recognises her own faults in him, but later realises that this has been a projection of her own feelings on to him, and it is a relief to find that he is not in fact like herself. This is a development on her part beyond the adolescent stage where simple relationships are forged by the like-mindedness of the individuals concerned. Here the liking arises from a recognition of contrast.

> If she had ever thought idly of friends she would have liked to have had, she would have imagined someone much more like herself, who shared her interests and shared her bent of mind. She wondered now how she could ever have found Ian Pollard like herself. He was a breath of fresh air to her with his positive practical drive and his outgoing warmth; it was such a relief to find someone who did not tie himself up in tight little knots as she did herself. (p. 112)

Such growth of understanding would normally result in 'love' or even marriage in conventional teenage fiction, but here it leads to friendship. She resists the interpretation of the gossips in the hospital that this is romantic love leading to marriage and children. For her that kind of love is out of the question because in her physical condition she could never be a full participant. When another patient mentions these possibilities to her she finds the whole idea 'grotesque almost abscene' — 'How could anyone wish to marry her except for the most perverted motives?' And for herself 'there could never be anything but the shadows of other people's lives watched in the magic mirror' (p. 116). She makes the point to Pollard, to whom she can talk about such things — 'There's something morbid, unhealthy, in wanting to devote your whole life to a woman who's crippled. It's not a natural form of love' (p. 142).

Pollard's response is to say that she has a lot to learn about love and about life. She cannot avoid human folk just by analysing her thoughts. The reality is that people in wheelchairs do get married. 'Someone will fall in love with you against his will, against his better judgement.' (p. 143). He is referred here to love as an irrational, uncontrollable force which may overwhelm her and her future lover.

As a statement of what love is all about, this has obvious weaknesses, but for Irene it is a necessary line to take. She has, in a sense, become too rational about her feelings and relationships, and she needs to know that one is not always fully in control of one's emotions. Her relationship with Pollard is a case in point.

What he partly represents is that half of herself which is in rebellion against the hospital, and it is through her dialogue with him that we see her attempting to come to terms with life in that institution. Just as *A Patch of Blue* is about a relationship against the backcloth of a racist society, *The View From the Window* deals with a relationship in the context of another form of oppression – the oppression of life in total institutions, classically portrayed in Ken Kesey's *One Flew Over the Cuckoo's Nest*. In comparison with the latter, however, the view of hospital life presented here is more ambivalent.

To see Pollard she has to break the rules – that is, leave the hospital premises without permission, but she can only do this if she believes that the rules and the institution that made them are 'senseless and intolerable'. Although she believes this to be true when she is in the act of breaking them, in her more rational moments she realises that some of the rules are reasonable, and in any case a person in her position – a regular visitor to the hospital, unlike Pollard, whose condition is temporary – has more to lose by getting on the wrong side of the nursing staff. She even feels a surge of loyalty to the hospital which is probably near to what Pollard describes as 'patient mentality'. Her ambivalent feelings towards the hospital are difficult to explain to someone not in her position. Everything has two sides to it. Even the mindless occupational therapy which she and the other patients are expected to do every day can be construed in a more positive way.

However, in the final analysis the anti-hospital view seems, in this particular instance, to win out. In a remarkable sequence we are shown the ward sister in her true colours – as a moralist in the guise of a pragmatist. Sister is commenting on Irene's general lack of enthusiasm for participating in activities along with other patients. She eloquently puts the institutional view:

> You must be aware that in a place like this where a number of people are shut up together week after week, all of whom have plenty of reason to be depressed, it is very easy for everyone to be miserable. It only takes one person who openly indulges in gloom and despondency – the mood soon communicates itself to everyone else. Most people realize this and do their best to be cheerful for the sake

of other people. (p. 127)

She does not feel Irene has made much effort here. She has adopted a superior attitude and not thought about the others. Thus she may have contributed to the demoralisation which it is part of Sister's job to avoid. She is after all supposed to be concerned with the psychological as well as the physical welfare of patients.

Irene is almost convinced by Sister and begins to feel guilty, but as she continues she begins to rant and Irene begins to see flaws in her reasoning. Beneath her tirade is a moralistic attitude, which finally surfaces — 'you have been having clandestine meetings with a man of what I can only call doubtful morals.' (p. 129). Rather than this being sensible advice, Irene quickly realises that it is 'mocked-up melodrama', and she is so furious that she at last openly rebels and gives Sister a mouthful of 'the crudest words she could think of' (actually not very crude!).

Underpinning Sister's pragmatism, therefore, is a moral judgement about her relationship with Pollard. Irene senses this, and thus her response: 'Before you let your imagination run riot, let me remind you that with my hips I am physically incapable of the act of copulation.' (p. 129).

Ultimately, what makes the hospital oppressive are not the rules and regulations themselves, but the moralistic stances of the members of staff who operate them. Were it not for them, we feel that Irene might have come to terms with the many other features of hospital life which she disliked. Even to hint, however, that there was something morally doubtful about her relationship with Pollard is such a gross intrusion on her privacy that she feels she has to make a stand.

The author has made an interesting observation here about the relationship between two principles on which most institutional rules are based. These two potentially conflicting principles are described by Hargreaves, Hestor and Mellor (1975) in their study of rule-breaking in classrooms:

> The first principle we shall call the moral principle. A rule can be established and justified by an appeal to this moral principle . . . Such rules and the values from which they are derived, are seen by members to be inherently 'right', 'proper' and 'just' . . . The second principle we shall call the pragmatic principle . . . Such rules appertain not because they are 'right' but because they 'work'. (pp. 221-2)

This study was written largely from the point of view of the teaching staff rather than the pupils. Cordelia Jones is impressing upon us that life in institutions is made even more oppressive for inmates and, in a sense, also for staff if moral principles are concealed beneath pragmatic ones in a way which is basically dishonest.

Jones's book clearly strikes a blow for the freedom of physically disabled persons to make relationships with whomsoever they wish, but although the thoughts and emotions of the heroine are explored in an interesting way it seems to me that the sexual side of her nature is not dealt with satisfactorily. She herself makes odd comments about incapabilities in this respect, and the outburst against Sister shows that it is something which has been on her mind. But why is the thought of sex grotesque and horrible? There are moments when the subject is broached, but the author seems to shy away from a more explicit treatment. When Pollard talks to her about 'love', for instance, it is in response to her 'condition', but it is an inadequate response because he does not suggest what sort of potential for sexual relations someone in her condition may have. If he wants to make her aware of the blindness of love, why not talk to her about her own sexual nature and that of the man who loves her?

In short, there is a germ of truth in Sister's assertion that she adopts a superior attitude, part of this being rooted in her suppression of her own sexuality. The 'ordinary' patients are not being 'grotesque' when they hint at a sex-based romantic attachment. They are being tactless and perhaps a little insensitive, but do not mean any harm. Irene finds their suggestive comments difficult to take because she seems to want to deny the sensuality of her being. The author skirts this taboo area and leaves the reader feeling that only half the story has been told.

The sexual and emotional needs of disabled people is, of course, a difficult area to explore, particularly in a novel written for young people. But, as Thomas (1982) points out, a climate has been created in recent years where such issues can be openly discussed, and it is now generally accepted that 'people with a disability require a sexual relationship as well as many other kinds of relationship' (p. 68). In the light of this, sex and the young, disabled person seems as legitimate a topic for the novelist as sex and the 'normal' adolescent.

A Screwball Covered in Daisies

The View From the Window makes an interesting contrast with Susan Sallis's *Sweet Frannie*, where the sensual nature of the disabled heroine is explored more fully. Fran is a sixteen-year-old paraplegic girl with a weak heart who is living on borrowed time. She agrees to take up the offer of a place in a residential home, but insists that the doctor in charge — Dr Beamish — tells no one about her true condition. She grows to love another inmate, Lucas Hawkins, an eighteen-year-old who has lost his legs in a motorbike accident and has withdrawn into himself. She helps him come out of his shell, mainly by needling him, which is her way of doing things. The relationship that develops, however, cannot lead anywhere because she knows that she could die at any time — a fact which she has to be reminded of by Dr Beamish. After refusing Lucas's offer of marriage, she confronts him with the truth about her condition.

There are some vivid passages describing her feelings about her body and her appreciation of sensation:

> I looked down and saw my arms. They were long and beautifully curved and already honey coloured. I stretched them in front of me and looked at the back of my hands; then I brought them slowly to my face, palm to palm, prayerfully. After that they moved by themselves, dancing slowly in the sunlight and with great significance like the hand movements of a Japanese dancer. I watched them with delight. They were leaves, they were butterflies, they were swallows and throbbing larks and spiky starfish. They were frail and then strong, helpless and very capable. They fluttered like snowflakes in the winter and struck swiftly like the rain on the sea. (p. 48)

She loves physical sensation. She loves smells and swimming. We are not surprised when she realises her love for Lucas is not just a mind and soul thing, but her body too is involved, 'my pulsating, beating body', despite her having no feeling below hip level on account of her handicap.

Her love affair is tragic, but like all good tragedies it does not leave us depressed. Fran has a great zest for life, which stays with her right to the end of her time. In fact, she is so bubbling over with life that she can even make a useful contribution to the survival of others, like Lucas Hawkins, whom she helps through a very black period. Not that this is a sacrifice for her. She gains from the experience because she has never herself experienced this version of love before. Previously she had got her kicks vicariously by bringing other people together like Dr Beamish and Nurse Casey. In fact, it was these little intrigues which kept her going. No doubt Irene of *The View From My Window* would have detested her for this, but would have admired her self-assertion and rebelliousness.

Fran could certainly keep the institution at arms' length. She stamped her personality not only on her room but the institution as a whole. She was mischievous and broke the rules, but the staff were more understanding than in Irene's hospital. There was no sitting back and observing through a window for her. She tried to make life happen and she was good for the other inmates. As one of them, old Granny Gorman, remarked, it was Fran's smart-aleck remarks that made her feel she was still alive.

Like many sensitive disabled people, Fran can spot a patronising attitude a mile off, which is why she is edgy with people like Aunt Nell and Uncle Roger — two friends of the hospital who make regular visits and occasionally adopt one of the residents. She perceives them at first as do-gooder types, spurred on by guilt, the 'sharpest goad of all', but later establishes a fairly positive relationship with them.

She prefers the blunt, down-to-earth, honest approach, which is why she gets on well with Nurse Casey, whose lack of bedside manner she admires! Nurse Casey just tells her to shut up and get into bed 'which is what she'd say to anyone whether they were paraplegic or not' (p. 7).

And because she herself so dislikes being patronised, her own attitude is completely free of condescension and this eventually makes her acceptable to Lucas Hawkins. But he is a tough nut to crack. Their relationship formally begins when she rings his number more out of curiosity than anything else. Their early exchanges are full of needle that goes beyond friendly banter. Hawkins says things to her that strike home — 'it was as if a knife came up from under my ribs.' The following conversation is typical. It demonstrates the author's punchy writing and reveals much about Fran.

'I've tried every damned number. Woken everyone in the blasted hospital . . .'
I said furiously, 'It's not a hospital. It's a home. It's our home.'
'Why didn't you say you were a patient? Wouldn't it have made things much easier.'
I screamed at him. 'I am not a patient Hawkins! You might be a patient, but I am not. I am a resident. Got that?' I waited a bit and thought of something else. 'And I don't want to make things easier for you boyo. I want to make them harder. Harder! Understand?'
He hadn't heard me . . . I sobbed. 'I hate you. I hate you because you need not be here at all. Because you've had everything you wanted out of life and now there's something you want more than

life and you're sulking because you can't have it!'

He went on reflectively. 'I think you're the screwball I saw when I arrived. Covered in daisies. I thought the place must be a loony bin.' (p. 38).

One of the book's ironies is that although Fran establishes this relationship with Lucas off her own bat, so to speak, it is one that Dr Beamish, Nurse Casey, Uncle Roger and Aunt Nell were hoping would happen, and indeed were even planning for such an occurrence behind the scenes. Fran, however, twigs this from an early stage. She is told about Lucas by Roger and Nell who suggest that she might help him to get interested in life again. Her response is typical: 'Do you mean I've got to seduce him? Don't you think that's tasteless to say the least? A paraplegic going all out for . . .' (p. 35).

Yet, although this is a clear case of manipulation by the institution, we do not resent it in quite the same way as we do the intrusions of the sister in *The View From the Window* because it is basically benign. In any case, from Fran's viewpoint the relationship was already underway as a result of her own initiatives.

Whether or not it was planned, we are left in little doubt that the relationship is mutually enhancing for Fran and Lucas. Fran's depressions have troughs as deep as those of Lucas. When she falls ill with pneumonia she opts for solitary confinement in her room for days on end, and obstinately refuses to do anything, even to come down for meals. The author provides us with an interesting insight into how depression is experienced. Fran develops a strategy for remaining immobile and self absorbed.

I sat there and set myself to thinking of nothing. They say it's not possible. Maybe not, but it is possible to think of a stone. A stone sitting on a lot of land — say, a desert. A dreary grey stone, nothing underneath it, no specially interesting shape. You can use up whole half-hours without having to resort to a book or another thought. I used up the morning and the lunch hour and some time after, and I got quite a kick out of it. Like some people with too much money get a kick out of burning fivers or standing on a bridge and ripping them up and letting them flutter into the water beneath. That is what I was doing with my time. I'd got a limited amount. Why the hell should I try to fill it any more? A pointless, exercise. I would waste it. (p. 53).

When she is in these moods even the abrasiveness of the well-meaning and dedicated Nurse Casey makes little impact on her. In the end it is Lucas who snaps her out of her mood with a phone call, just as she had rung him when he was low. Life just will not leave either of them alone! Their concern for each other is a reflection of the strength of the emotional bond between them. Fran will not be allowed to fritter away her remaining in socially useless self-absorption.

It is this mutuality which prevents the relationship being just another case of female self-sacrifice. Even after death her memory lives on in him, and the thought that this might happen must have helped her at the end. She has always wanted to leave her mark on the world. She has 'welded' her room to her 'so that even if I died tomorrow it would be Fran's room' (p. 12). And now her lover has provided her with the possibility of immortality. Her impact on him has been profound. He has known her for only five months, 'hardly any time at all, yet a life time. Almost nothing, yet everything' (p. 96).

Although they are treated differently in each book, *Sweet Frannie* and *The View from the Window* have at least two themes in common. One is to do with the tension in a female personality between what might be called the cognitive/rational and the affective/irrational, and the resolution of this tension in a way which does not reduce the young woman to emotional dependence. The second related theme is about the creation of space within institutions which will permit personal identity and positive human relationships to flower.

Strength Through Writing

Both these themes are brought together in a different form in a powerful book for older readers called *Nineteen is Too Young To Die* by Gunnell Beckman, translated by Joan Tate. This is the story of Annika, who discovers that she has leukemia and knows that she has not long to live. Like *Sweet Frannie* it is a novel about facing up to death. Annika's strategy is to lock herself away in the family's deserted summer cottage and write about her life, partly to make a record, but also to maintain a grip on reality as she struggles to retain her dignity by not allowing the toad

which is sitting hiding in my chest . . . to blow itself up and fill up the whole of me . . . spurting out its horrid anxiety-venom into all my veins and cells. Forcing me to weep again and again, idiotic,

uncontrollable weeping . . . like a disappointed child who has been
forced to go home from the party before all the fun is over (p. 10).

At first the writing is barely coherent, but she does not give in to
hysteria. She plods on through long, rambling sentences, nonsense-
writing and a multitude of spelling errors to some semblance of
control over the thoughts and emotions which, to put it mildly, had
knocked her off balance.

Unlike Fran, she does contemplate suicide, but is sufficiently concerned about her nearest and dearest not to go through with it. At first,
she considers its attractions. It would make everything much simpler
both for herself, her mother and her boyfriend Jacob — 'I wouldn't
have to listen to that horrid, cheerful, strained, neutral note in their
voices' (p. 28). However, she remembers what her Gran once said
about those who were nearest never being able to forgive themselves, and it might remain on their consciences for as long as they
lived. In any case, she is too much of a coward. Also, deep down, there
is a lingering hope that a mistake might have been made or that a
hitherto unknown remedy might be discovered.

A great deal of her writing is about Jacob, her boyfriend, which
inevitably also involves writing about her mother and father who are
divorced. The writing is not just for anyone. It is for an old girlfriend
called Helen, who performs the role of *alter ego*. She imagines Helen
telling her to pull herself together.

The historical period is more explicitly indicated here than in most
of the other novels discussed in this chapter. The time is the late
1960s, the boyfriend, Jacob, is very political and very dominant. Of
course, she is writing about her relationships of a previous period when
she did not know she had leukemia. It is interesting that whole sections
of the book could probably stand on their own as a valid account of a
young girl growing up, irrespective of whether it was written by a
heroine who now had leukemia or one who did not have such an illness.
However, the fact that it is written from the point of view of someone
with a terminal illness generates an urgency in the style which cuts
through trivia and enables the reader to feel that he or she is being
taken to the heart of the matter.

From Annika's perspective it is her illness which produces the need
to write, and the writing itself produces its own form of truth. She
remarks at one point that the words when written become independent
— 'sometimes better than what you intended sometimes worse'. Writing
produces its own truth because one always adjusts words and facts to

the receiver, just as 'one writes one's own diary and then adjusts it for the reader who is oneself' (p. 99). It is this kind of insight which the reader feels makes writing a therapeutic process for her. She is clearly being taken out of herself by words.

She met Jacob after he had taken his degree and just after he had returned home from India. She reflects on how he threw open the door to a whole new world for her and her mother. She became swept up in the radical politics of the times, and was plied with literature about emergent countries, race relations, woman's place in society, Vietnam and the Middle East. Her mother, who was a doctor, became so committed that she went off to Pakistan to work in a hospital for Oxfam. Annika went to live in Stockholm with her mother's cousin Agnes, a liberal, but not radical enough for Jacob, whose offer of marriage was really only a solution that he favoured to the problem of where she should live. It is this kind of behaviour of Jacob that prompted her to think more deeply about her relationship with him. She did not realise at the time that that was the 'beginning of some kind of wakening'. She thought she loved him, but unlike the conventional heroine she queried what this 'love' actually meant.

I do love him. If I now know what 'love' is at all, that is. It's such a gigantic word which you fling around so lightheartedly, you read and hear it all over the place and it's taken for granted that you know what it means just like 'eat' or 'think' or 'run'. (p. 4)

Her interpretation is interesting. She feels completely happy in his arms 'Perhaps that's because then we . . . how can I explain it . . . then we're equal — at the same level, or something; oh, it's so hard to express — mostly because I don't really understand it myself' (p. 40).

Like many other experiences of 'love', there is an emotional blinding, a confusion, but the meaning she is grasping for is clear. It is not a simple question of emotionalism or irrationality. There is thought built into the very experience of love which reflects the values and cultural preoccupations of the times. In her case, she does not love him because she wants to possess him or feel dependent on him or because she just cannot help it, but because in the act of love she achieves a sense of equality which is missing from the rest of their relationship. Normally, the relationship is dominated by him — the strong one, mature, 'so full of knowledge, so certain of himself'. But she is happiest when she feels equal, instead of feeling that she is being modelled by him. Gradually, however, she discovered 'that I was just like a stuffed doll' who knew nothing about herself. She began to see faults in Jacob. The most annoying thing about him was that he was not really interested in her experiences. When, for example, she told him about a book she had been reading, with a trivial-sounding title but important to her, he dismissed it with 'I think I've got some rather more important litera- ture to read'. When she showed him a story she had written about her experiences in an old people's home, he infuriated her with his patron- ising remark 'That's a really moving little story'. It is at that point that she began to admit to herself that she did on occasion actually hate him. She was critical of the lack of balance in his personality between thought and emotion, which was at the root of his inability to link his reactions in personal relations with his political views, which in turn led to all sorts of contradictions. For example, he supported equality on a societal but not apparently on an individual level. Annika summed it up neatly, without completely dismissing the need for cognitive awareness:

> He knows lots and lots about poverty and starvation and the suffer- ing of the world and all that, but sometimes it seems to me that the suffering never actually gets under his own skin. It's as if saving the world were just a rational research assignment. And I suppose it has to be that. You'd never get far with just sentiment. (p. 49)

Jacob was also not interested in her thoughts about her father. Had he ever met him, he would probably have dismissed him as a reaction- ary old fuddy-duddy. It was a self-defeating attitude because it failed to probe individual consciousness, and therefore impeded his arriving at an understanding of what sort of radical political message might potentially appeal to people like Annika's father.

In short, what the author has managed to convey so simply and clearly is the political mood amongst many 'new left' radicals of recent times which has been characterised by a preoccupation with the complex issue of the relationship between the 'personal' and the 'political'. The heroine's criticism of her boyfriend's traditional political attitudes and her understanding of the need for attention to be given to the problems of consciousness and emotional life are rooted in her experience of a personal relationship. The author's account via the heroine reflects an astute political awareness rare in writers for children and young people. When reading the book one is reminded of passages in political commentaries like the following by Zaretsky (1976):

We need a more tentative and experimental attitude towards emotional life. We should realize that feeling, intuition and sensation have their own special value, and their own limitations, just as rational thought does, and that the kinds of personalities we've developed, particularly our one-sided emphases on either thought or feeling, are the result of particular forms of historical development. (p. 142)

Her father's story reflected human weakness as well as sheer bad luck. It is when she is nursing him through an illness that she gradually gains insight into his character as someone totally different from herself or Jacob, someone who is near to having been completely crushed by failure. He failed his university exams, was sacked by the newspaper that employed him, was left by his wife, produced manuscripts that publishers were not interested in — all of which could objectively be attributed to circumstances beyond his control; but even though he knows this — 'one is a product of one's heritage and environment and all that' — he still feels that he could have made better choices and blames himself for not having done so. He has now grown cynical and tired of life. He talks to her about his loneliness and about death, and expresses his views on the younger generation and politics. He admits to being a 'stuffy old reactionary', because basically he cannot do anything else in his condition.

Don't you see . . . no, of course you can't see . . . that you have to make peace with yourself to be able to be interested in others. And I'm one of those people in this wonderfully fortunate country who can't afford to have a world conscience. (p. 77)

There is, of course from the reader's viewpoint, plenty to argue with here. Maybe it is the case that he cannot afford *not* to have a world conscience. But Annika does not take this up. Instead, she asks for his forgiveness. Her conversation with her father has enabled her to see that becoming a radical is not quite as straightforward as both she and Jacob imagine, and that some people are reactionary not out of 'badness' but because they are too busy patching up their own tent to worry about other people's. Nevertheless, it is essential to sustain communication with such people, because it is likely that you will always be able to offer them something. She in fact manages to interest her father in the comforting verses of a modern female poet. Moreover, she gets something from the relationship too — 'an anchorage, knowledge —

solidarity' (p. 82) which is an outcome of an abstractionist like Jacob would not have anticipated. In splitting emotion from cognition one is perhaps limiting one's imaginative range. This has been forced on father through circumstances, but for Jacob there are no excuses. It could perhaps be said of Jacob what Annika's father said of her mother — 'It's dangerous not to have an imagination because you can hurt people without meaning to simply because you don't understand.' (p. 102).

It is because she knows that Jacob lacks imagination that she anticipates with trepidation their first meeting since he has known about her leukemia. The gap between them will be even wider because 'there's a kind of chasm between the healthy and the sick'. But she is determined to forget everything that separates them. In a sense, her illness has given her a kind of strength. She feels less vulnerable and therefore more willing to surrender herself to his embrace. The ending leaves the reader with a puzzle. Is it possible that Jacob has drowned. Is it possible that she may be cured?

This is a novel about growing up which gets away from the usual format of the adolescent adapting to a *status quo* over which they have little influence. Annika queries the personality of her boyfriend in the way that many female characters would not. They would accept their dependence and his dominance. She has become conscious of the need to establish her own identity, which paradoxically her illness helps her to do, and to construct her own definition of reality from the bits and pieces that come through to her from other people. She does not just adapt to society, but society also adapts to her.

The same is true of Fran in *Sweet Frannie* and to some extent of Irene in *The View From the Window*. Fran makes life happen and changes life in the process. When she refuses to do O-level courses we can see that this is possibly a mistake, but also that her view that it is a waste of time could be valid for her. Her attitude towards 'society' is that it needs her as much as she needs it. This is typified by the following exchange between her and Dr Beamish: ' "When I read your file I knew you were a screwball Fran. I think we might be glad of you." I said vigorously, "Glad of me? Christ, you need me!" ' (p. 28).

Similarly, Irene's speaking out against the oppressive attitude of the ward sister is part of her personal statement against the existing structure of hospital life.

Teenage Girl Must Have Boyfriend

This is completely the opposite of the view taken of adolescence in Myra Schneider's *If Only I Could Walk*. I have chosen to discuss this book because it is an example of many in this genre which sit uneasily between conventional romance like *A Wind Is Blowing* and the social and psychological realism of a novel like *Sweet Frannie*. The author, in trying to present a view of a disabled adolescent as having the same sorts of problems as any 'normal' girl of her age, works with a definition of normality which is questionable to say the least. The normality assumed is one where the adolescent gets it wrong until they are put right on the nature of reality by those who are older and wiser. Thus, Penny, the sixteen-year-old *spina bifida* heroine starts with an unrealistic view of the world. She has left school to take up a course in shorthand and typing at the local college, but what she would really like to do is work in some capacity for the BBC. Her sister lets her know in no uncertain terms what is wrong with this aspiration:

> 'They train people who have already got qualifications, you nut, people who have done A-levels and courses. You've got nothing and yet after two days at that college you've decided you won't bother with shorthand and typing even though this course is your big chance to get a qualification. It's time you came out of dreamland, Pen, and woke up to reality.' (p. 46)

Her friend Cindy also has a go: 'The trouble with you, Penny Carter, is that whatever you're doing you always want to be doing something else.' (p. 56).

Society has her pretty well fixed status wise, and the message is that the best thing she can do is accept this. She is not without intelligence — after all, she is good enough to go to college, but clearly not a high-flier who is likely to get A-levels. It is partly a motivational problem with her. Parts of her school report run through her head reinforcing the jibes of friends and relatives — 'You're wasting your talents, Penny, you give up the moment anything's difficult' (p. 56). Social-class wise she comes from a background which is low but not bottom rung. Her father is in charge of a greengrocery in a supermarket. When she eventually applies herself she realises that she *can* learn the shorthand signs. She is neither very clever, nor stupid but somewhere in between. Adapting to society means accepting this view of her intellectual status. She may think typing and shorthand are boring, but this is clearly not to be taken seriously because girls like her can make very good secretaries. This may be so, but in the event of no other option being suggested, the reader is being asked to agree that this is the most sensible outcome and probably the best she can hope for. There is something predetermined about her adaptation to social life. Like all adolescents she makes mistakes. For example, she mistakes the friendly attitude of Dave, the boy next door, for passionate concern. She likes him because he 'said things straight out all the time' and he is honest about his position in life. In a way they are both in the same boat. He has no qualifications, and his prospects of getting a job straight after he leaves school are poor. If anything his social background is a notch lower than Penny's. His father is a van driver who goes straight down to the boozer after finishing work. Educationally he is also inferior to her. He does not obtain one job he applies for because his reading and writing are not good enough. Her fantasy that he is romantically inclined towards her is punctured, when she finds out that he has being going steady with another girl. At first she does not want to believe this, and deceives herself into thinking that it is all over between him and this girl. She is naïve enough to think that 'Love Dave' on the bottom of one of his letters is proof that he 'specially cared' about her (surely not credible?). She is, of course, hurt when she finally realises that Dave's relationship with this other girl is relatively permanent.

But this is typical of Penny. She is full of teenage fantasies. In her case, fantasies about boys are sometimes related to her disabled condition. She pretends, for example, that her sister Maureen's boyfriend has a twin brother called Bill who is also a medical student, and whose ambition is to spend his life curing conditions which prevented people from walking. On the other hand, underneath it all, she is afraid that her disablement will prevent her achieving her aspirations for a relationship with a 'normal' boy. Her fantasies are not healthy because they are rooted in repressed feelings of despair, and a deep sense of inadequacy, more profound than the normal inferiority feelings of adolescents. She is, after all, *spina bifida*, confined to a wheel chair, unable to feel anything from the waist down and has to wear a plastic bag because of incontinence. It is not that she does not face up to this. She does in her own way and in some ways her version of reality is as valid as her sister's. She wants things to be different, that's her dream; to have a normal boyfriend, and indeed why shouldn't she dream this? But she knows how things stand — 'Why don't you speak the truth' she says to Maureen 'I'm too handicapped to have a boyfriend' (p. 77).

Maureen's response, for once, is more optimistic. There are good things about 'reality' as well as bad. This time Maureen's version of the truth is more palatable for Penny. But the reader should note how Maureen in fact slides away from the issue that really concerns her sister. 'That's tripe, you've as much right to a boyfriend as anyone else.'

Penny looks at her unbelievingly, but why should she do this? The question of her right to a boyfriend is not the issue. It is not her right that she seems to be bothered about, but whether or not she will actually be able to have a boyfriend. The reader feels that Penny should not be taken in by Maureen's specious argument, which continues:

Listen Penny. You've got to face your handicap and how it will limit you, but you've also got to get it out of your head that the world is divided into two sorts of people: the able-bodied who can walk and have all the goodies in life and the handicapped who are stuck in wheelchairs or blind or whatever and have to go without any goodies. There are thousands of people about who look normal but have incredible problems. (p. 78)

Penny begins to see the sense of this, but rather than 'reality', isn't it only a partial truth, no more valid than her own more pessimistic view on the topic? Society does in fact divide people in this way. 'Normals' do get more 'goodies' than the disabled. It is true the 'normals' also have problems, but can many of these really be compared with the permanent and intractable problems faced by an adolescent girl with *spina bifida*? The point surely is not that she should ignore these realities and agree with her sister, but that she should acknowledge their existence and fight for the right to have as many 'goodies' as the able-bodied. Maureen's tendency is always towards placing the blame on Penny's attitude, but it is the attitude of the rest of society, we feel, which is just as much at fault.

On a deeper level, however, we can question whether these 'goodies' themselves are so desirable. The conservatism of this book lies in the way existing priorities are taken for granted. Both Penny and Maureen share the traditional view of the importance of boyfriends, sex, marriage and children. Penny thinks she cannot have them, Maureen says she can. But Penny is being asked to adapt to a world where she is bound to be at a disadvantage. Of course, there is nothing wrong with someone like her having sex and boyfriends, but why should it be so central to her existence when she does not have an equal opportunity in

the market where there is such fierce competition for these overvalued
commodities? If Maureen was really being helpful she should encourage
Penny to appreciate alternative values, ones that exploited her strengths
rather than her weaknesses.

Ultimately, it is Penny who is in fact more realistic, even though
neither the characters nor the author seem to acknowledge this. When
she is advised not to get too fond of Dave she thinks the implication is
that a girl like her should 'make do' with someone who has also got a
problem — someone, for example, like Gordon, a friend she met at
college, who has a bad stutter and therefore, in her words, 'good
enough for someone who can't walk and whose body doesn't work
properly' (p. 57). She tries to resist being typed as someone whose
range of choice of boyfriends is restricted to a ghetto full of boys with
problems.

But she does end up with Gordon, despite her sister's denial of the
division between able-bodied sheep and handicapped goats. And it is a
very positive relationship. They help each other overcome inhibitions
rooted in inferiority feelings. After an initial reluctance, she becomes
very close to Gordon both physically and emotionally. They hold
hands, kiss and she feels extraordinarily happy. She knows Gordon
will understand the full extent of her handicap — plastic bag an' all.

We are asked to believe, however, that this is not the ghetto relationship which she originally resisted. Gordon's caring for her sparks off
a sense of belonging 'to life itself'. But this sense of belonging is merely
an adaptation to the *status quo*. She has a new outlook, but nothing has
really changed in the direction she wanted it to — a direction which she
had a perfect right to follow and which would have involved an emergent critique of existing arrangements. Of course, we know that she has
to adapt to Maureen's reality because that is the dominant view of the
way the world is, but she does not have to be extraordinarily happy
when Gordon kisses her. Looked at objectively, her course is still boring
and her boyfriend still has a problem. Both these things she had wanted
to avoid, for understandable reasons, but she ends up coming to terms
with both of them.

Summary

The first book discussed in this chapter — Edwards's *A Wind is Blowing*
— typifies the way disability is often portrayed in male/female relationships in adolescence and young adulthood. The girl is devoted to her
disabled boyfriend who, apart from his disability, which in any case is
only temporary, has many 'positive' attributes. In fact in marriage-

market terms he is a highly desirable commodity – handsome, well off and intelligent. They are, of course, 'in love'.

In the rest of the chapter books are reviewed which, in different ways and with varying degrees of success, attempt to get away from portraying relationships between disabled and 'normal' characters within the traditional teenage romantic novel format. In Kata's *A Patch of Blue* it is the heroine who is disabled, and neither she nor her boyfriend come from enviable backgrounds. She is permanently blind and disfigured as well. The book has many strengths, but the growth of love between the two central characters is assumed rather than demonstrated in a convincing way, and the book ends on an ambivalent note.

Jones's *The View From the Window* makes the notion of 'love' more problematic. The disabled heroine thinks more deeply about her feelings for an older man who is also disabled, albeit temporarily. This book also contains interesting insights into the experiences of a disabled person living in a residential institution which she needs from a medical viewpoint, but in which she feels restricted and put down. However, sex and sensuality are not dealt with openly enough in this novel, a fault it shares with some more conventional forms.

The latter is certainly not true of Sallis's *Sweet Frannie* where the sensual nature of the disabled heroine is fully explored. Although she spends the last few months of her life helping a boy, a fellow inmate, with whom she has fallen in love, this is not just another case of female self-sacrifice. The book has a great deal to say about love, sex and disability; life in institutions and facing up to death at an early age.

This last theme is also dealt with in Beckman's *Nineteen is Too Young to Die*, a novel for older readers. This is probably the least conventional of all the books discussed in this chapter. The heroine may be adjusting to the fact that her own life is going to end, but the discoveries she has made about her own identity seem to represent a beginning rather than a finale, a dawn of a new era where women are considered the equal of men and where personal relationships as well as political systems are radically changed. This novel makes an interesting contrast with Schneider's *If Only I Could Walk*, where the heroine who has *spina bifida* eventually comes to terms with rather than challenges the *status quo*.

8 CHILDREN AND DISABLED ADULTS

The Warnock Committee recommended 'that there should be more opportunities for people with disabilities to become teachers and obtain teaching posts in both special and ordinary schools' (para. 12.75). The appointment of such teachers is, of course, desirable in its own right in a society where disabled people are often discriminated against, particularly in relation to job opportunities. But such teachers can also make a unique contribution to the cause of the disabled by providing examples of 'handicapped' persons who are living normal lives despite their special difficulties, and who are not self-centred and preoccupied with their own problems but outward going, and just as concerned about the welfare, growth and development of their pupils as any other teacher.

We can expect children's attitudes towards disabled adults to be as diverse as they are towards disabled children. They will be influenced by myth and legend, media portrayal and half-knowledge from their own limited experiences. Again, literature has provided a collection of stereotypes which are undoubtedly partly responsible for negative attitudes amongst some children. In children's fiction the disabled adult has often been portrayed as an embittered and menacing character who, like Long John Silver, seeks to manipulate children for his own evil ends, or as a man bearing a grudge against society, who uses his distorted body or artificial limbs in a sinister and aggressive fashion, e.g. Captain Hook.

In this chapter I shall discuss books in which the disabled adult is portrayed as a character who does not arouse fear and suspicion in children, or at least if he does, it is only temporary and shown to be unwarranted.

Coping With An Emotionally Crippled Father

In Bernard Ashley's *Dodgem* the disabled adult is too mentally disturbed to be a threat to the child hero. In fact, he is a pathetic character who is totally dependent on his son. Since the death of his wife in a car accident Mr Leighton has been virtually a zombie, and has been looked after with great care and dedication by his son Simon.

It was no wonder Simon was never at school. Some of the more insensitive teachers at school did not understand that this was not just ordinary truancy, and that Simon was in fact behaving very responsibly. On the rare occasions he was at school he was continually worrying about what his father was doing at home. If he turned the gas fire on, for example, would he remember to light the flame? Such worries naturally had a deleterious effect on his performance at school, but he doubted if his teacher could see that there was any difference between himself and other kids in trouble.

No, it just wasn't the same for him, and that wasn't being soft, that was a straight fact. No mother, and a father who'd changed after she'd died from being the best signwriter around – a real artist– into a zombie who sat and stared at the wall, and picked at his fingers, and had to be bullied into eating enough to keep himself going. And him the one who was doing the keeping going. No, there was a difference, even between himself and the other kids in trouble; and if she couldn't see that, she was stupid. (p. 13)

The pressures were on him at school and at home where Alex, his father, was extremely trying to live with. Every little upset was a major tragedy. If he broke a couple of saucers, he would 'be standing there staring at the damage as if the broken crockery was another death.' (p. 21).

Yet there were events that made Simon more hopeful, that suggested that Alex was trying to respond to the great efforts his son was making to liven him up and bring him back into the real world. The glimmer of hope is well observed by Ashley in the following passage. Simon hastens to the kitchen when he hears a crash and finds Alex with broken crockery all round his feet. He had been preparing the tea. As Simon stoops to pick up the pieces he realises that Alex had actually considered him:

'Hey!' Simon stooped to the china; he wasn't looking at the floor; he was staring at his father; Plates? Swiss roll? Alex had never got cake out before. He'd manage a cup of tea but that was it; even getting out a packet of biscuits was beyond him. Today, though, he'd gone to the cupboard for the Swiss roll; Simon's favourite.

An end of the cake fell from Alex's grip, and rocked a piece of china to and fro. It was absurd, the throttled, breaking cake and the uncertain face of his father, looking as if he were a dog caught with the Sunday joint.

'Cake's off then,' Simon said. He looked into Alex's eyes. It was impossible to expect him to smile: anyway, who wanted to smile today? But somehow that wasn't the important thing. The point was, for the first time in nearly a year Alex had done something off his own bat, for him. (p. 22)

The emotional tone here is very similar to that in *Welcome Home, Jellybean* and *What About Me*. Like Neil or Dorrie, Simon is watching out for signs of humanity in a person living what superficially appears to be a vegetable-like existence. The feelings involved in *Dodgem*, however, are even more complex. Simon does not just want to communicate for his father's sake, although that is part of it. He wants to communicate so that he can understand his father's role in his mother's death. At the back of his mind is the nagging thought that his father, who was driving the car at the time, was in some way more responsible for the death than the term 'accident' implied.

One of the book's main subtleties revolves around Simon's going through experiences which help him to understand his own burgeoning emotions, and, as a result of this, to arrive at a clearer understanding of just what might have been going through his father's mind at the time of the accident. But the portrait of Simon is not one of a lad under pressure being driven by impulses to behave in this way or that. His behaviour may seem bizarre, stupid and lacking in reality awareness, but the author unlocks his personality in a way which enables us to see him as a rational, purposive human being. He may be 'maladjusted' in a technical sense, but he is not disturbed.

Given the basic assumptions that guide his actions, his behaviour is perfectly rational. He must run away from the residential assessment centre (where he has been placed by officialdom as a result of his truancy and the situation at home) because he does not see his or his father's needs being met in institutions. He plans to escape, collect his father from the mental hospital, and to get out of London so that they can lose themselves somewhere in the country. This rather naïve plan is made a practical possibility by a Mr Penfold, a fairground traveller, whose resourceful, worldly-wise daughter Rose has befriended Simon in the residential home. Fairground people required signwriters and painters, and Penfold decided that he could exploit Alex's talents, which were beginning to return as a result of his treatment in the hospital. The children make their well-planned and brilliantly executed escape from the home; Alex is collected from the hospital, and with the help of Penfold and Rose they merge into the fairground community. It is his relationship with Rose which provides Simon with the experience which helps him to resolve some of the problems which have been on his mind. He experiences sharp feelings of jealousy when he sees Rose flirting with other boys and men, an unexceptional activity as far as Rose is concerned – just part and parcel of fairground life – but he is hurt by it. On reflection, he realises that it is not Rose towards whom his angry feelings are directed so much as the men she is flirting with. He deduces from this that if his father had deliberately intended to kill anybody it would have been his mother's dancing partner rather than his mother herself. His father was clearly jealous of her being with other men, but would never have killed her on account of that.

The relationship between Simon and his father is well contextualised in a world where welfare institutions are dominant and are part of what Simon wants to escape from, in order to find a personal and social space where he and his father can live out their lives. In fact, the alternative is just as impersonal and more seedy and exploitative. In the end, the welfare institutions do not come out of all this too badly, although there is a lesson here for them. Teachers and other professionals should be more sensitive to the needs of such children. Simon himself voices his complaints about school, and also his fears about the residential assessment centre

> The real world lost its hold on you after a time and about a week was enough to do it, it seemed. They didn't need to watch him at night anymore. He was feeling defeated and the terrible thing was that he was coming to terms with it (p. 88)

and his opinion of his placement there –

> Marvellous, wasn't it? Simon thought. The Welfare thought one of the reasons he wouldn't go to school was he couldn't face up to the bullies. So they sent him somewhere where it goes on all the time. They put him in the aggro here to make sure he goes to school to put up with the aggro there. It seemed a crazy sort of thinking. (p. 44)

When Simon had attended school, he was subjected to bullying by a particularly nasty couple of bullies, who used to goad him about his mother: 'Bit of a tart, your old lady, weren't she Leighton?'

There are some brilliant cameo-like, mildly satirical portraits of
social workers, like Rick at the assessment centre 'Hi, I'm Rick' – and
the education welfare officer – 'a man who knew how to get across a
threshold.' But even Simon is forced to admit that the centre does have
its good points –

> In lots of ways they'd been marvellous to him at the Lodge. Rick
> had had long talks with him, taken him out in the Transit to collect
> some laundry, walked in the grounds with him and talked about
> Alex and his mental illness. (p. 88)

Simon learns a great deal about himself and his father, and about
the bruising environment in which they struggle to survive. The book
shows how it is possible for a lad in his early teens to cope with difficulties of which writers with a more patronising view of childhood
would not have thought him capable. He can come through partly
because of inner strengths, but also because the welfare framework,
despite its faults, does provide a safety net in the end. Simon himself
is a child of the modern age – surviving in a complex environment
by various devious means; and coming to terms with himself and
his father by thinking through his problems in a rational way. This is
how we would like to think 'deviant' children are motivated.

A Man Full of Locked Doors

Paton Walsh's *Goldengrove* is another novel where a young person is
portrayed in a caring role in relation to a disabled adult. Unlike
Dodgem, this story is set in a more exclusive and tranquil world than
the one Ashley describes. Goldengrove is the home of the heroine
Madge's grandmother, and is situated in its own grounds near the sea
in Cornwall. The beach that Madge visits is virtually their own because
'the only way down to it lies over Gran's land' (p. 8). Madge is no
Simon. She is a high-flier with an 'English examination' mind which
enables her to think of an apt quote from literature whenever she
requires one.

The book has many faults. The plot is rather fragmented, and
different parts of the story appear to have only a tenuous connectedness.
Also, the way lower-class people are portrayed is questionable, which
is important bearing in mind what has been written earlier on this
point. Madge, although sympathetic to the blind professor Ralph, is

herself blind to her privileged position. Her grandmother has a cook-cum-maid Amy, who has a boyfriend called Walt from the American airbase and who calls Madge 'Miss'. Madge has no qualms about accepting this form of address. There is no attempt on her part to establish rapport with the maid, as, for example, Mary Anne does in *The View Beyond My Father*. She supposes that Amy is 'sulky' because she is left with all the dishes every day, but there is no suggestion that she herself might give her a hand occasionally so that she can get off early! Jeremy, the local fisherman, is also portrayed as something of a fore-lock-touching character, who asks after Miss Madge and (her brother) Master Paul 'all summer, every time we send down to him for mackerel.' (p. 30).

However, the relationship between Madge and the blind professor Ralph does have some interesting qualities. She is introduced to Ralph by Gran. She finds his conversation abrasive and stimulating. She is fascinated by him and offers to read for him. The fact that he is blind enables her to stare at him 'as you never could at anyone else' and she compares his face 'crowded, full of events, for all the blankness of his eyes' with her own and Paul's, which are 'empty as the open air.' During their conversations he conveys to her his feelings about people being kind to him. This comes as a surprise to Madge:

'I don't know that I like people being kind to me,' he says.
'Why ever not?' she says astonished again. 'I like it lots.'
'Well for lots of reasons but mainly because they stop sooner or later just when you've got used to it.' (p. 41)

Madge, however, in her lady-bountiful way is prepared not to stop. Although he claims not to need kindness she does not see why she should not come to read to him. He takes on a handsome appearance as Madge falls for him in typical adolescent fashion — 'He is my Rochester and I am his Jane.' As she becomes more involved with him he also takes on a more fatherly image. He teaches her a great deal about the experience of blindness. In one moving passage he asks her to read from Milton, and she wonders how he can bear to rub salt in his wounds; but he explains how reading Milton on his blindness helps him to 'objectify'. Madge does not understand, and so he explains.

'It means to put things outside me. Makes them into objects, external to the mind . . . Another man's pain, against which to measure one's own. A scream to put against one's own silence. It helps me to grasp how much of what I am is blindness and how much is me. (p. 78)

She can relate this to her experience of the day before, when she had experimented with trying to walk around the house without sight after getting Paul to blindfold her.

As the relationship develops we observe them becoming closer, and sense that Ralph is giving off signals which suggest that Madge is getting through to him. He asks if he can touch her and she allows him to explore her face with his hands. Madge responds to this gesture. She puts her arms around his neck and kisses him swiftly as she rises and moves away. These touching moments are described with great delicacy by the author:

He tilts her chin upturning her face towards him, and covers her over with both his hands outspread. His fingertips press gently on her temples, run along the line of her eyebrows, across the lids of her eyes, weighing them down, and lingering at the outer corners. His cobweb touch weaves over her, finding the shape of her cheekbone, and the turn of her jawbone, tracing down to her chin, running to and fro across her lips, and then he seems to have done, and holds her still, hands cupped round her chin. (p. 105)

Yet there is a certain ambivalence about this scene which in retrospect gives it an unexpected edge, because we know by the end of the book that Ralph remains an emotionally wounded man who restrains whatever affection he might hold for Madge. Like Alex in *Dodgem*, his defensiveness and withdrawal are due to the memory of the pain caused by the loss of his wife, although in this case it was the result of her leaving him rather than dying. This is compounded by his losing his sight during the war. In the end, he reveals that he cannot trust Madge. And for her this is a very chastening experience. It makes her realise an important truth. Although blindness is bad, it is not half so bad as being so defensive that one cannot trust or love someone. This dawns on her in a powerful moment at their final meeting:

'Oh Ralph,' she says dismayed. 'Something much worse than going blind has happened to you!'
'What could be worse?' he says morosely.
'Something worse has! You are full of locked doors marked No Kindness and Reading Voices Only and not letting people help and

not believing they will!'

'Madge, some wounds cannot be healed, some things are beyond helping and cannot be put right. That's just how it is.' (p. 114)

The book has rather a strange ending with Madge nearly succeeding in drowning herself after she learns that Paul is not her cousin but her brother. She is hurt by the knowledge that she has been deceived for so long. She had wanted a brother badly, but now it was too late for her to benefit from it. Suddenly, she understands what Ralph meant. 'Ralph had said things couldn't be mended, some things were too late to be put right. And I just thought that sounded sick and wicked, I didn't understand what he meant at all. But now I see.' (p. 124). So Madge's childhood passes, and a blind man helps her to lose her innocence. In retrospect the touching scene is symbolic of this.

It is interesting to compare the emotional depths plumbed by Paton Walsh in parts of this book with the superficiality of the Cleavers' *The Mimosa Tree*. I shall discuss this briefly as an example of a book which shares at least one important theme in common with the *Goldengrove* and *Dodgem* − child hero or heroine adopting a caring attitude towards an old disabled person − but which fails to present an adequate portrait of the main relationship or the character of the disabled adult. What makes these other books worth reading is that the adult is not a fixed, unchanging entity − handicapped and nothing but handicapped − but a living human being whose character is developed and whose relationship with the child is detailed for the reader.

The Mimosa Tree is the story of the Proffitt family, who leave a dirt farm in North Carolina and travel to Chicago where they hope to find a better life. Unfortunately, things do not work out for them. Mother deserts the family, father cannot find work because he is old and blind and has lost the will to work anyway, and the family drifts into poverty and a reliance on the promise of welfare. Marvella, who is at fourteen the eldest offspring, finds a job with a pawnbroker, but she has to give this up because she is too young. Her younger brother starts to steal, and most of the book is taken up with describing how life gets generally worse and more corrupting for the family as a whole. The mimosa tree is imaginary. She describes it to her father as part of the scene from the window of the flat in order to keep him relatively happy. Eventually, Marvella, who is now in charge, decides that their only hope is to return to the dirt farm.

The blind father is portrayed as passive and downtrodden, and figures little in the plot. He is a doubly oppressed man − economically broken because the land on the farm was too poor, and physically reduced by blindness. He has clearly given up. Marvella is the mainstay of the family. She reflects on how her father looks old for his age and how he no longer really understands what his children need. At one point she tries to enliven him with the hope that his blindness might be treatable, but he does not even wish to grasp at this last straw. The move to Chicago seems to make him even more withdrawn — 'Lately Pa was a little on the foolish side. The fix they were in hadn't seemed to sink in on him. All he did was dream of things past and talk about things that weren't real.' (p. 65).

In fact, there is a suggestion in the text that he understands more than Marvella gives him credit for. Just as they are about to leave Chicago she confesses to him that the mimosa tree does not really exist. His reply is unexpected: 'Well I didn't see how they could. This air ain't fitting for anything to breathe. I'm glad to be going from here. We all set?' (p. 105).

But if there really is more going on in that old head than we surmise, why haven't we been told more about him? A character is hinted at but does not emerge from the shadows.

The Growth Of Trust In Rural Communities

Two well-known books for middle years children in which disabled adult characters play prominent roles are DeJong's *Journey from Peppermint Street* and *The Wheel On The School* by the same author. These are more concerned than the books discussed so far with the positive contribution such adults can make to community life. In both we see people of all ages — the young and the old — working together towards common goals, and enjoying themselves in the process. The barriers to communication between age groups, and between 'normals' and disabled people are broken down.

The journey from his home in Peppermint Street to the monastery in the marsh where his Aunt Hinka and deaf-mute uncle live is an adventure for Siebren in more ways than one. He is accompanying his grandfather, who is visiting his dying sister and who has traversed the ground many times before, but for Siebren it is a new and powerful experience. He has to relate for an extended period to adults other than his parents. For him the journey is full of surprises requiring him to use his limited experience to the full, and in the process of doing so he learns a great deal about himself and the nature of adults. We see how adult behaviour can be confusing and baffling for a young child with a mind only just emerging from the influence of magic and super- stition and guided by non-adult priorities and significances. He ponders on things his grandfather tells him and tries to make sense of them, often getting the wrong end of the stick, as children do.

At times he wonders whether he has been lied to, and this is an important issue because it is a test of whether or not he can trust these adults in whose charge he has been temporarily placed. When Aunt Hinka leaves a stone in place of her hand as he drifts off to sleep, he suspects that she has, for some reason, attempted to deceive him, but realises that she has only done this in order that the removal of her hand would not wake him. It was done, in fact, in his interests, and he realises that there is no ill-intention or dishonesty involved.

In general, his trust in and admiration for Aunt Hinka is unwaver- ing, which is more than can be said for his attitude towards Grandpa, whose puzzling behaviour stretches Siebren's capacity for understand- ing to the full. He realises that Grandpa is fallible when, disregarding his own advice, the latter goes wading into the swamp. But that, Siebren acknowledges, is what all adults are like – there were elements of inconsistency even in the most consistent of them. They were changeable, but this did not mean they could not be trusted. Grandpa was sometimes stern and strict then teasing, then fun, then wonderful.

Adults could help the young sort things out mentally and emotion- ally. Siebren feels safe enough with Aunt Hinka to tell her about his fears and guilt feelings. He fears he might be a 'handball of Satan' because he spoke to himself, because of what he supposedly had done to his brother Knillis to make him non-communicating, and because of the mistake he had made in locking up a stray dog in a place where it might have starved to death. Aunt Hinka reassures him on all these points, but does not let him off lightly.

Of course, Siebren knows that not all adults are like this, and there were some who clearly did tell him 'anything to get rid of him' and who could not be trusted, but he has learnt to trust Aunt Hinka, and it is largely her support he relies on when anticipating with tre- pidation his meeting with the tall giant of a man, the deaf and dumb Uncle Siebren, in whose charge he has been left by Aunt Hinka.

Siebren soon realises that he has nothing to fear from this uncle of his. He is a character of great gentleness who communicates through gestures and by writing. He leaves a simple, friendly, note for Siebren, which has a touch of self deprecating humour – it is from the 'biggest, deafest, dumbest uncle that you ever saw.' (p. 164). Siebren observes how he 'talks' to Aunt Hinka with his fingers.

Uncle Siebren, like other adults in this story, is portrayed as more than just a friendly adult. He helps the young Siebren to achieve insight into his brother Knillis's needs. When he observes his uncle using finger language he thinks that this might be a useful way of communicating with Knillis, who could not say anything but 'Da'. But his uncle knows that this is not really an appropriate strategy. Forthrightly, but without talking down to him, he puts him off the idea. 'He wrote, "For Pete's sake why? If he can speak one word he'll speak all words in time. And you can speak – so why, why in the world?" ' (p. 189).

But Knillis seemed so lacking in ability. All Siebren could do was build blocks for him to knock down. This elicits from Uncle Siebren the following insight:

'Then build blocks for him – if it seems forever. Build them for him to knock down. You *want* to knock things down when you can't talk. But while you're building blocks talk to him. Talk and talk and talk – then after a while your little brother will talk too – if only to stop your everlasting talk' Uncle Siebren grinned. (p. 189).

An important theme explored in this book is the nature of the way adults talk to children, each adult having his or her own style of talking to Siebren in a manner which does not insult or demean him. And this ultimately is in the adult's interest as well as the child's. Both Grandpa and Aunt Hinka have to depend on Siebren at certain points in the story – a Siebren growing in confidence and understanding as a result of the way adults have treated him. This mutual dependence can therefore be a feature of all positive child/adult relationships, not just those involving a 'normal' child and a dependent disabled adult. Understanding and relating to such an adult is only a variation of relationships with all adults – disabled or not. Of course, there are special features, e.g. learning to talk with fingers, and disabled adults may appear strange and even arouse fear at first; but such difficulties can readily be overcome if the child is accustomed to trusting adults. A pathological fear of disabled adults would probably be indicative of a 'faulty' perception of adults generally. In DeJong's gentle story we feel that the unsophisticated but salt-of-the-earth adults are fully aware of a child's needs in this respect.

Like *The Journey To Peppermint Street*, the *Wheel On The School* is a long, rambling novel, perhaps, too long for the age group. The legless Janus is feared by the children because of his reputation. He did on one occasion actually thrash a child who attempted to steal cherries from the tree he guards obsessionally. A social isolate who spends a great deal of time worrying about his property (his wife even brings him stones to throw at invading boys and birds), he is not the sort of person one would imagine participating in a community enterprise.

Yet the children find his assistance invaluable when they are seeking help with their project — a project aimed at getting storks to nest on the roofs of houses in their village like they did in other villages. Although he is legless, he is strong in arms and hands. He helps the children retrieve a wheel from the sea in dangerous circumstances, and to put a wheel on top of the school for the storks to nest on. We observe him becoming socially confident enough to joke with everybody — children and adults alike — about his disability. Janus eventually becomes so involved with the project that he leaves behind his unproductive, property-conscious existence to become a fully fledged community member. His wife, Jana, understands the change that has taken place.

> There he sat like a king among the excited, chattering boys. After a moment Jana looked down at what she was doing. Her fingers in her pocket were rooting among the smooth stones that she had picked up along her bread route that day. They were extra smooth and round, extra special ones for Janus to throw at birds and boys. She pulled them out and looked at them. One by one she dropped them at her feet. (p. 181)

The children now feel they can trust Janus, and he is in a position to help them. When they read a report on the likelihood of storks perishing in the storm, it is to Janus they turn for reassurance. He queries the accuracy of the newspaper report, and tells them that storks 'are too smart to be caught over water in a storm' (p. 242).

This is an old-fashioned tale looking back to a time when it was possible for the young, old and disabled to be active together as members of the same community, when there was a difference of perspective between the generations but not an unbridgeable gap, and when people could be snapped out of their preoccupations with self by the enthusiasm of the new generation. There is integration for all here, of which integration of the disabled is a part, and there is warmth in the relationships established which positively glows in both DeJong's novels. Yet this is the world as it was rather than how it is now. As such it is a valid statement on life then, but for modern children it does not have the same relevance as a book like *Dodgem*.

Summary

Handicapped adults have often been portrayed as embittered characters who arouse fear and suspicion in children. The books with which I have been concerned in this chapter counter this stereotype. In Ashley's *Dodgem* the emotionally crippled father of the hero is a pathetic figure whose rehabilitation is facilitated by the efforts of his loyal son, Simon. The question of fear is not significant, but Simon could easily have despised his father. Instead, the caring side of this young truant is revealed. He has his suspicions, but these constitute a problem with which he struggles and finally resolves to his own satisfaction. Simon might be thought of as 'disturbed' himself, but his behaviour is perfectly rational in the circumstances. He is Welfare-wise, and a 'deviant' of the modern era.

Dodgem is set in a bruising, modern, urban environment; the remaining stories (apart from the Cleavers' *The Mimosa Tree*) take place in more rural, idyllic settings. Paton Walsh's *Goldengrove*, though set in beautiful scenery, has some harsh points to make about the personality of the blind adult character and his relations with the heroine, Madge. This is no conventional portrait of an embittered disabled person, but nevertheless his personality does have a darker side to it which Madge later discovers.

DeJong's *Journey From Peppermint Street* and *The Wheel On The School* both contain disabled characters who strike fear into children when they are unknown to them, but whose warmth, humour, friendliness and usefulness eventually come through and are appreciated by the children. An important theme in both these books is the growth of trust between children and both disabled and able-bodied adults. They have clearly been written for a younger age group than *Dodgem* or *Goldengrove*, and have a nostalgic quality.

FOR YOUNGER CHILDREN

The rather cumbersome expression 'quasi-fiction' has been used for books which are written in story form, but where the main aim is to convey factual information about the disability or difficulty. The plot in such books is usually very thin, sometimes almost totally non-existent, and they tend to rely on pictures. Most of them are difficult to classify as fiction or non-fiction. Some are clearly more one than the other, if one considers each of them in terms of a continuum between two modes of discourse, but generally there is enough of the fictional element in most of them for them to be included for discussion in this book.

In this chapter I want to begin by discussing three books, each of which represents a different point on this continuum. These and most of the other books discussed in this chapter are intended for younger children, pre-school, infant and early junior. There is a paucity of information on how children at these ages react to books of this kind, and I do not propose to make any generalisations about actual or possible responses. However, in order to help clarify the argument presented, I have made use of some empirical material in the form of a mother's comments on her four-year-old son's reactions to the books.

The first and most factual book is Paul White's *Janet at School*. Janet is a *spina bifida* girl who attends an ordinary infants school. We see her taking part in many of the usual activities of school life: hanging her coat up, painting, doing puzzles, reading and even using the gym apparatus in the school hall; and, at home, the kind of activities that one might expect in a 'normal' family situation: messing about on the piano, playing lego in the company of brother, sister and dad, helping with the washing up, having a meal and going on holiday. The main aim is clearly to impart information about *spina bifida*. On one page there is a drawing of a human figure showing the skull, spine, thigh bone and bones of the lower leg with an explanation of the *spina bifida* condition. The illustrations are a series of colourful photographs depicting scenes at school, home and camp, and arranged in a sequence giving a rough indication of a typical day in Janet's life. The illustrations are accompanied by a text of average length for a book of this type, although employing a vocabulary beyond the reading abilities of most

Figure 9.1

Jane was very proud of her inhaler. She used it every day and soon she began to feel better.

five-year-olds.

The second is about a girl with asthma – *Jane Has Asthma* by Nigel Snell. This is more of a story than *Janet at School*. Jane is sad because she doesn't feel like running about with her friends in the park because of her difficulty with breathing. Mum takes her to the doctor who listens to her chest, administers various tests and gives her a 'little machine' – an inhaler – and some medicine to take away with her. She begins to feel better and the story ends on an optimistic note – one day she will be able to run about like the other children. The illustrations are simple, brightly coloured line drawings of the type often found in comics (see Figure 9.1).

Freddy Bloom's *The Boy Who Couldn't Hear* has a much stronger story line, although the text is briefer and simpler than in *Janet at School*. On the first page we find Mark, a deaf boy, fishing by himself in a river. Some boys nearby get angry when he splashes them with his net, but he cannot hear what they are saying and runs off to find Mum. She takes him back to the river and explains to the boys about deafness. She explains about his hearing aid and lip reading. When he arrives home he tells his Dad that he has left his fishing net behind. The next day he has a lesson using a speech trainer (see Figure 9.2). When Grandpa comes he brings a surprise present — a fishing rod — and later at the river when accompanied by Dad his new friends turn up. They have found his fishing net.

Figure 9.2

Next morning Mark had his special
lesson using the speech trainer.
It is like a very strong hearing aid. 25

In her notes on her little boy's responses to *Janet at School* the mother wrote that 'he didn't really know how to respond at all'. There was some mild curiosity as to how Janet became like that — 'Did it break?', 'Maybe something in the mummy's broke it' (sic). Paradoxically, in view of the documentary nature of this book, the initial reaction was that it wasn't 'real life truth' at all, but was looked upon as a fantasy — a typical response perhaps of a child who could not relate the material to his own experiences. In general, the book was not liked.

There was a more favourable reaction to both of the other books. In response to *Jane Has Asthma* he said 'I like this 'cos it's funny' and when questioned further referred to the park keeper getting cross, the children's facial expressions, and incidental features like a clock with Mickey Mouse hands and an advertisement on the back of a bus. In relation to *The Boy Who Couldn't Hear* the mother wrote 'he quite liked this', and she felt his comments suggested the beginnings of an awareness of some of the difficulties a deaf child might encounter.

The key phrase here seems to be "cos it's funny'. Even children at this age may be put off by blandness and like their characters to have an edge to them. They may like them to be humorous or cheeky, or at least to have interests like fishing with which they can identify.

The interesting thing about Mark is that he is portrayed as a boy who is keen on fishing. He is a boy who is concerned about fishing nets and fishing rods and who happens to be deaf. We can believe in the genuineness of his interest because we see him being worried about the fact that he left his fishing net behind when he ran away from the boys (see Figure 9.3), and we observe him being delighted by Grandpa's surprise gift of a fishing rod. Of course, all this is very thinly sketched, but represents an important developmental line in the character of Mark.

A more rounded portrait of the disabled character is also attempted in *Jane Has Asthma*, although the whole story is more centred on asthma than the previous one was on deafness. She feels sad and later begins to feel better, because of the things that happen in the story. There is an unfolding of events which lead to an alteration in her emotional state. In contrast, Janet of *Janet at School* 'likes' this and 'enjoys' that but there is no indication of her emotional development. We observe her engaging in one activity after another, but learn nothing about what really amuses her or really interests her. Janet does whatever is put in front of her to do, as if the only thing that mattered was that she did the same things as other children. We would like to know more about her reactions when, for example, her younger sister

Figure 9.3

At home Mark remembered that he had left his net behind. "Never mind," said B

interferes with her games. We would like to know how she feels about this problem and to observe how she comes to terms with it. We see fragments of her life, but we do not see her living through an experience as we do with Jane or Mark.

It would be inaccurate, however, to suggest that any of these books was particularly interesting to our four-year-old reader. His mother observed that when given a choice he did not spontaneously select any of them. She felt that in some ways even at this age-level they were too basic and not sufficiently stimulating, and that the authors would have done better to have made 'much more of a story to it'. Yet, at the same time, she did not feel that the information contained in the stories was explanatory enough.

It seems to me that there is a danger these books may fall between two stools. In trying to impart information and tell a story they do neither very well. Perhaps there is too much of the wrong kind of factual information. One of the aims of the books is presumably to show that disabled children have their loves and laughs, and differ only from other children in so far as all individuals differ to some extent. They have their ups and downs, happy times and sad times just like every one else. The presentation of facts must surely be subsumed under this main aim, and as far as possible must be integrated into the story in such a way that it is not interruptive of plot development. Whole pages, for example, devoted to explaining away deafness can be a turn-off for a young child who wants to get on with the story if a story is what he or she has been led to expect.

Another point concerns the language used in the books. It is often not clear for whom the book is intended, but even when younger age groups are clearly being addressed the language is bland and impoverished, similar to that used in the worst kind of basic reader. There is no sense of the author trying to make reading fun in the way that Bettelheim and Zelan (1981), for example, suggest, i.e. bearing in mind that children like playing with language, require words that stir the imagination and like the feeling of words on the tongue. Language can be brought alive by using the first person or in picture books by placing words in speech bubbles. Bettelheim and Zelan are, of course, referring to earliest reading books, but a similar point can be made about these stories which are intended perhaps for an older age group of younger readers. Compare, for example, this passage extracted from *The Boy Who Couldn't Hear* with one from a book by Ezra Jack Keats, *Apt. 3*, where the author is clearly aware of the importance of the poetry of language.

Mark was born deaf. One afternoon when he was fishing, some boys were angry because he was splashing with his net. 'Hey, stop it!' Mark couldn't hear what they were saying but he saw they were angry and was frightened. (*The Boy Who Couldn't Hear*, pp. 7–11)

Sam went into the hall and listened. No music.
His little brother Ben tagged along.
Sam listened at the door across the hall.
Crunch, crunch, crunch.
Crunch, crackle, crunch!
Someone – or something – turned the knob. (*Apt. 3*)

In addition to language and characterisation, another important feature to consider is the degree to which the book's values are consonant with the integrationist philosophy which is my major concern in this book. Lively language and interesting characterisation do not preclude the possibility that such positive features may be used to reinforce notions about children with disabilities which impedes rather than enhances their acceptance in the ordinary school situation. The child may be asked to regard them, for example, as characters from what amounts to a separate culture from his or her own and therefore 'naturally' segregated by language and personality into their own 'special' establishments.

All the books discussed so far try to avoid doing this and aim to inform and demystify the disability for 'normal' children. Yet it is important to note that explicit aims may not be realised because certain implicit features of the book may negate them. So that, for example, even though integration is the key theme of *Janet at School*, heavily emphasised in the pictures as well as the text, the fact that Janet's personality does not really come across means that she may remain outside the experience of the other children and therefore unknown to them as a person in her own right whom they can relate to. Children know that because a child plays alongside you in teacher-organised activities or eats dinner next to you it does not necessarily mean she is your friend.

Other picture books are even more clearly integrationist in intention than these three. In Elizabeth Fanshawe's *Rachel* the little girl does not even do her artwork in a separate corner of the room as Janet does, but sits at the same table as her 'normal' peers and seems to share their experiences (see Figure 9.4). She also makes a useful contribution to the classroom chores, like feeding the gerbils and cleaning up after art lessons. The final picture is of Rachel in assembly singing along with the rest of the children, the handles of her wheelchair barely visible.

In *Suzy*, by Elizabeth Chapman, a partially sighted girl of junior school age is seen leading a full life at an ordinary school and at home. Her special difficulties are not ignored, but we see how they can be overcome without any elaborate arrangements. She sits with her friends reading and talking, a book with large print propped up in front of her. She obtains a special magnifying glass for reading — no sacred tool but one that her brother can casually borrow to look at his stamps. She has a friend called Chrissie who informs her of the number of a bus that is arriving at the bus stop. Like Rachel, she seems to want to act as an independent and socially useful person. We see her taking initiatives like deciding to give the clay rabbit she has made at school to Mr Barton,

Figure 9.4

an old man she has befriended. This is in response, perhaps, to what he has given her — his time and an opportunity to play with his racing pigeons.

Both these books show children with disabilities leading reasonably normal lives in ordinary schools. In both there is a sense of the disabled heroines beginning to take responsibility for their own lives, and one can imagine them becoming independent and valued members of the community.

The same cannot be said, however, of some other books which, if anything, seem to reinforce a segregationist view of the education of children with disabilities. In Palle Peterson's *Sally Can't See* the 12-year-old blind girl goes to a residential special school and does not come home until the end of term. No explanation is given as to why the school should be residential or why she cannot stay at home with mother and father, and the implicit explanation as to why the school has to be special is not convincing. For instance, most of the activities which she engages in could be just as easily carried out with appropriate arrangements in the ordinary school — swimming, athletics, cleaning out the budgie, riding, etc. And the specialist activities — feeling shapes of lions, numbers and countries — seem to be at too low an educational level for her. For a girl who when at home in the holidays goes shopping on her own and who is learning to play the organ, feeling large numbers and animal models is surely a task which is well below what she is capable of? Is this perhaps an indication of the lowered expectation often complained of in relation to special schools? We see her mixing with other blind children. She has a sighted friend with whom she seems not to do much other than 'walking out together in the sunshine'. She appears only once, right at the beginning of the story, and we hear nothing more of her.

Althea's *I Use a Wheelchair* is another book where it is taken for granted that a child with a disability will go to 'a special school where most of the other children are in wheelchairs'. Judging from the text, this is a book for children who are a year or two older than the audience aimed at in *Rachel*. Although right at the end there is an indication that the heroine *may* be going to an ordinary school, there is no build-up to this. For instance, the girl never says that she is unhappy at her special school or that, although she is happy, it has certain disadvantages. We see her getting involved in activities such as playing hockey with other wheelchaired children (see Figure 9.5) and having speed trials on sports day 'strapped in our wheelchairs'. Swimming and horse riding are mentioned, but we do not see her actually engaged in

Figure 9.5

these more 'normal' activities. In fact, there are no pictures of her engaged in sporting activities which do not involve wheelchairs. She has other friends, but mostly she seems content to mix with other disabled children. Her experience of 'normal' children – 'children giggle and point at me' (see Figure 9.6) and her brother's footballing friends who 'laugh and say I don't play properly' – is clearly at the root of her apprehensiveness about the prospect of going to an ordinary school. 'I'm a bit scared about how I will manage. I think other children will be a bit scared of me too.'

It is worthy of comment that a book like this should have been published in 1983, and thus at a time when one can point to many examples of physically handicapped children who have been able to cope successfully in the ordinary school. Compared with *Rachel*, published eight years earlier, it seems far less forward looking. Maybe this reflects a change of opinion amongst disabled people themselves? A controversy certainly exists of which one should be aware even if there is not space enough to explore it fully. There is no doubt that children in wheelchairs do have something in common, both in the physical

Figure 9.6

sense and in terms of the oppression they share when insensitive 'normals' laugh at them or call them names, as in *I Use a Wheelchair*. But although there is clearly a need for solidarity amongst the disabled, there is also a need to avoid the elaboration of policies which confine them to a ghetto. Thus although, just as in the case of ethnic minority groups or women, one would support the formation of pressure groups to further the interests of those who are discriminated against in our society, this does not imply that one would agree to the continuance of a separatist education.

Another book about which I have misgivings is Althea's *I Have Diabetes*. Diabetes is a difficult disability for younger children to appreciate, for the obvious reason that it is not visible in the way that some other disabilities are. It is also difficult to understand because it cannot easily be described except by using a technical vocabulary beyond the range of most children for whom picture books like this are intended. I am thinking of words like blood sugar, insulin and pancreas gland, which have to be understood in some way before the child can appreciate what the problem is.

In this book there is clearly a concern to confront young children with the truth about diabetes — to dissolve some of the mysteries surrounding it and thus pave the way for a greater understanding of the needs of children with diabetes. Of all the books discussed so far it is probably the most forthright and explicit. There are pictures of the girl injecting herself (like the heroine in *I Use a Wheelchair* she does not seem to have a name), checking her urine and blood-sugar level and keeping a record for the doctor. She behaves sensibly and has clearly acquired some medical knowledge about her own problem. She adopts a rational approach and shows no fear of her condition, the treatment or the doctors who help her. She even manages to explain, albeit in a way that a young child would probably have difficulty understanding, the meaning of 'hypo'. The matter of fact tone is typical of the book.

'I always keep some glucose sweets in my pocket in case I go 'hypo' which means there is not enough sugar in my blood. I usually know because I start feeling grumpy, and do silly things. Sometimes I feel dizzy or shaky and go hot and cold. I sit down and eat some sweets and usually feel all right quite quickly. I might faint if I didn't have them.

I sometimes go 'hypo' if I race around without eating something first or if I am late for a meal.'

And yet one wonders if children reading this book will obtain from it the message intended. There is one particularly striking picture of children at a holiday camp for children with diabetes. They are all, at the same time, injecting themselves with insulin, having interrupted their picnic in order to do so (see Figure 9.7). One can, perhaps, see the reasoning behind this portrayal as far as diabetes sufferers themselves are concerned. The holiday camp may have an educational and training aim. For children with diabetes from social backgrounds where there is a lack of concern for hygiene or an appreciation of the importance of establishing a routine of self-administered treatment, a holiday situation might provide an opportunity to teach good habits. But if this is the aim of such camps it is not conveyed in the text. The child reader could easily assume that this is not just an arrangement for a selected group of children with this problem, but that diabetic children generally would be expected to go on holiday with their own kind in camps especially designed for them. Surely, this is labelling at its worst? It

Figure 9.7

Last year I went to a holiday camp
for children with diabetes.
I learnt to ride a horse and
we went on lots of picnics.
I hope I can go again this year.

gives the impression that such children are so different that even their
leisure time has to be organised.

Another aspect that it is essential to consider when evaluating quasi-
fiction is one that has been discussed in relation to several other books
in the previous chapters. The question should always be asked: To what
extent does the book avoid incidentally reinforcing other divisions in
society which are not ultimately beneficial to children with disabilities?

For instance, an important consideration is how the parental roles
are portrayed in families with a disabled offspring. A book which is
progressive in this respect is White's *Janet at School*. There are several
pictures of Dad engaged in various domestic activities, e.g. washing up
and playing with the children; and Janet's upbringing clearly involves
both parents, not just Mum. In fact, the book may go too far with
Mum being pushed into the background, but perhaps this is justified
in view of the imbalance which has existed in previous literature, where
the mother has played the prominent role and father has hardly parti-
cipated at all. Father was the bread-winner who came home to his
newspaper and a nice dinner cooked by Mum.

In some of the other books the authors are clearly sensitive to this issue, but often do not handle it very well. In *Rachel* both parents play an active role, but there is one picture of the family at meal time where the accompanying text reads 'Daddy sits next to me', which seems to suggest a friendly enough father, but one whose attention is special and not just routine like mother's is. It is as if father's generosity is remarkable whereas mother's is expected, as if, therefore, one is more valued than the other because it comes from an unusual source.

In general, however, most authors of recent quasi-fiction portray fathers as involved as mothers. Some also include black children amongst the 'normal' children in the story (e.g. *I Use a Wheelchair*), and children who giggle or tease or get angry do not seem to come exclusively from one particular social class. Most families are of the nuclear type — Dad, Mum and kids with a Grandad and Grandmum visiting — but some are clearly single parent families, e.g. Peter's *Claire and Emma*.

Another point to bear in mind is the age range for which these books are appropriate. Although the pictures make them accessible to younger children this does not mean that older children or even adults cannot gain something from them, particularly if they are unfamiliar with the disability. On the back cover of *I Have Diabetes*, a person with diabetes writes: 'I am sure this book will inform diabetic children, their friends, families, teachers and anyone else interested in what it means to be diabetic.'

Clearly, the audience aimed at here is much broader than one might imagine from an initial persual of the text. This is a worthy project but it does mean there is a danger of the books falling between several stools and appealing to no one. P. Wilson's and S. Irvine's *If You Knew Nicky* is a case in point. This is a short book with glossy photographs about an autistic boy, Nicky. The foreword is clearly intended for the adult reader, and is a simple explanation by a psychologist with a string of letters after her name about this 'rare and mysterious childhood disorder'. There is an above-average amount of text accompanying the pictures which seems to make it more suitable for a junior age child, but one wonders if even a child of this age would understand what was really the matter with Nicky? His behaviour is supposed to be mysterious (even the experts themselves, as the foreword acknowledges, are baffled by this condition), and yet superficially no one piece of behaviour in itself is particularly strange from a child's viewpoint. Many children play with the same thing over and over again, sometimes, if not all the time, and sometimes 'normal' children are awkward and do not like to be cuddled.

Some picture books are clearly aimed at older children and their parents and these are often the most successful. Marshall's *Mike*, for example, is a beautifully illustrated book about a boy in his early teens who suffers from nocturnal enuresis. The various possible causes are sensibly and simply discussed with Mike himself by Dr Shah, who tells him that some children wet the bed when they are unhappy or worried, while others sleep so deeply that they cannot wake up in time to go to the toilet. It is at this point that Mike reveals to the reader as well as to Dr Shah that he is afraid of the dark and admits that he has not told anyone about this in case they thought that he was a baby. The book is written in the first person, but we are not told of these fears before his conversation with the doctor. In this way the author reinforces the point that Mike has kept it a secret because he was ashamed to admit it.

The explanation provided by the doctor helped to reduce what at first seems an insurmountable problem down to a size that can be handled by Mike and his family. One can imagine a teenager who has this problem being helped by reading this book. The most encouraging aspect would be the way the doctor's role was perceived. This is an excellent portrait of a doctor who does not patronise his young patients, but is willing to see them on their own unaccompanied by parents and chat to them about their problems in a relaxed, adult way (see Figure 9.8).

Another positive feature is the way the question of ridicule and shame is dealt with. Unlike some other problems, there does not seem to be much point in revealing all to the children at school. This seems to reflect the author's awareness of the realities of the peer-group situation. Mike is left at the end of the book feeling pleased that his friends at school do not know about his problem. I think the author's judgement is correct here because, although one could argue that the best outcome would be peer acceptance of his condition, the reality is that they would be unlikely to take the problem seriously. It is enough that he comes to terms with it himself. After all everybody is entitled to privacy, and there is no good reason why his problem should be made public. 'Coming out' as an enuretic is obviously not the same as declaring that one is epileptic or diabetic because the latter are more permanent and more likely to involve other people at some point. The technical side of Mike's treatment is accurately described — the rubber sheets, wall charts, pad and buzzer — and the book

Figure 9.8

After a bit, I told him that I was afraid of the dark and that I was scared to get out of bed at night. I hadn't told anyone in case they thought I was a baby.

is informative and well organised. The illustrations are apt, and the language in the text not as bland as in some other books in this genre. Altogether, this is an impressive attempt to convey an understanding of the psychology of a boy whose problem, though typical, is rarely dealt with in children's fiction. The hero is allowed to retain his dignity and pursues his normal activities at home and at school.

Finally, I should like to end this chapter by pointing to two areas which I have not touched upon because they did not strike me as very important, but which I am willing to have second thoughts about (!) and which the reader in any case may wish to consider further. Both of these might be considered in terms of their potential for generating useful research topics. First, the role of illustrations has not been dealt with in any great depth. I have made passing reference to this, but I must confess to having no particular view on the matter. It does not seem important to me whether pictures are photographs, line drawings or 'arty' pictures, provided that they are reasonably stimulating in one way or another — either in the sense that they convey interesting and useful information or that they are evocative of mood. Clearly, one has one's own opinion as to a picture's quality, but I personally find the gut reaction involved here too difficult to put into words. The reader may feel, however, with some justification, that when evaluating picture books it is crucial to examine the illustrations with great care, and in this he or she is in line with the thinking of many writers and illustrators who have been pursuing research in this area. I should say in passing that most of the research that has been done has used outdated, experimental methodologies to arrive at unsurprising conclusions, like, for example, that children's preferences for style depend on their previous experience of that style! This comment by Cianciolo (1978) on two research studies is typical:

> It is apparent from these studies that children's preferences for illustrations are due in large measure to the illustrations they have been exposed to in picture books which are read to them or which they read themselves; also the extent and content of the instruction about art in general or book art in particular which they have experienced. (p. 108)

What is clearly required here is a reconsideration of methodology in the direction of a lesser concern with attempts to be 'scientific'. I would have thought 'illuminative' research could have been carried out on this topic using alternative techniques, such as case studies and qualitative approaches, which are more compatible with the subject matter.

Secondly, I have not attempted to back up some of my impressions of typicality with the findings of empirical research partly because I wanted to concentrate on clarifying issues rather than making generalisations, and partly because very little relevant research has been carried out. However, some generalisations have inevitably crept into the discussion, and the reader must make his or her own mind up as to whether or not they are plausible as they stand. I would tend to agree with the reader if he or she felt that the writing would have been more persuasive had it, at certain points, been grounded in more empirical data. The sort of data I have in mind would be similar to that generated to support allegations of sex and race discrimination in basic readers and reading schemes. Some relevant research has been done here but not much. For example, Hopkins (1982) reports a study involving an examination of the most recent editions of twelve major basal reading series for references to handicapped individuals. The basal readers consisted of a number of selected stories, and the research was concerned not only with pre-primer and early readers, but all readers up to sixth grade. Of 4,656 selections only 39 stories (less than 1 per cent) dealt with any type of handicapping conditions. An analysis of 39 stories revealed that (a) there was nothing about handicap before third-grade level; (b) in five of the twelve basal series, stories about handicap occurred in only one of the dozen or more texts in the series, and it was thus possible that a child might be exposed to only one story about a handicapped person in six years at school; (c) blindness was the handicap represented in 25 of the 39 stories; (d) all other handicaps were represented by eight selections. The researcher points out that since other research has shown that children begin to discriminate against the physically handicapped by the age of four or five, not introducing a disabled character until the third grade was leaving it rather late. The researcher also comments on the fact that the high proportion dealing with blindness does not reflect the relatively low incidence of that particular disability.

Of course, such research begs many questions, not least the one which is my main preoccupation, namely that quality should also be considered along with quantity. In fact, in fiction for older children and juveniles, the problem is not the dearth of books with disabled characters so much as the amount of poor-quality literature in this area. However, such research has its place and needs to be kept up to date.

Summary

A number of quasi-fiction books have been reviewed, and it was felt that even for young children the disabled character should be portrayed as having interests and experiences (in addition to those specifically associated with his or her disability) with which a 'normal' child could identify. Unfortunately, most of the books fell between two stools. They did not have much of a story line, nor did they impart factual information very well. In addition, the language used tended to be bland and impoverished, and in certain cases it was also doubtful if the message of the book was consonant with integrationist philosophy. Some of the books, for example, took for granted that children with certain disabilities would automatically go to a special school or would require other forms of segregationist provision.

A similar point can be made about quasi-fiction as about the novels discussed in previous chapters, particularly in Chapter 4. To what extent does the book avoid reinforcing other divisions in society in a way which is counterproductive as far as children with disabilities are concerned? For example, most of the books discussed here reflect the author's sensitivity to sexist issues, such as the equal participation of both mother and father in the bringing up of a disabled child.

Although space in these books is more taken up with pictures than text, some of them are clearly aimed at older as well as younger age groups. Marshall's *Mike*, for example, is about a boy in his early teens who suffers from nocturnal enuresis. This book has many positive features and is one of the more impressive of what is not on the whole a very successful genre.

The chapter ends with a brief discussion of two areas where further research might be carried out. First, the role of illustrations is still something we know very little about and further work on this would be useful, provided a methodology was used which was more appropriate for the topic. Secondly, up-to-date surveys of basic reader and reading schemes are required similar to those carried out in relation to sex and race discrimination.

10 CHOOSING AND USING THE LITERATURE

In this chapter I want to conclude by making some observations on choosing and using the literature. In the first part, by way of summary, I want to draw out from the discussion of themes and issues a number of questions which teachers might like to ask themselves when considering the suitability of a book. In the second, I suggest an approach to teaching fiction which is in my view compatible with the general argument of the book.

Choosing the Literature

Is the Book Basically Pessimistic or Optimistic?

It is a convention that writing for children must have a happy ending in one way or another, so that the child reader is not left in the air, so to speak, having to grapple on his or her own with negative emotions and dark thoughts. In some books this happy ending seems too contrived. It is not a credible development of the story line or a way to end the book which is faithful to the characters involved. Such an ending is often justified on the grounds that writing for children should be basically optimistic. I would not quarrel with this as a moral imperative, but I would argue that writing for adults should be equally optimistic, and that whether a book has a happy ending is not a sufficient criterion of its optimism or pessimism.

Most of the books discussed in the foregoing chapters occupy an interesting position in relation to this issue. Although many of them clearly exude an air of optimism, the endings in most cases are certainly not 'happy' in a conventional sense. Most of the books referred to in Chapter 2 end on an ambiguous note, leaving the reader in some doubt as to the outcome of the situation. In Rodowsky's *What About Me?* the disabled character actually dies, but the ending is both sad and happy because Fredlet lives on as a cherished person in the memory of Dorrie. Even in Shyer's *Welcome Home, Jellybean*, which has a happier ending, we still feel that life is going to be a long haul for Neil, Geraldine and the parents. The tragic element is permanent, and no amount of rationalisation and adaptation can alter this basic fact of their existence.

However, although disability as a topic — and particularly, perhaps,

154

mental disability — is inherently difficult to treat in an optimistic fashion, it can be done, not so much by concocting a happy ending or by anticipating better things to come, but by infusing the story with a profound sense of the humanity of the disabled character. This is what happens in *Welcome Home, Jellybean* and to some extent in *What About Me?*, but not in Walsh's *Unleaving*, which I found a most pessimistic book. Neither do the human attributes of the disabled character come through in Brown's *The Siblings*. It is mostly via the attitudes of the 'normal' characters that a sense of optimism is conveyed. We either see through their eyes, or we do not, the worthwhileness of a life.

How is the Disabled Character Portrayed?

There are several points here which should be considered. First, the description of physical appearance clearly needs to be handled carefully. As I mentioned in Chapter 2, the evocation of traditional stereotypes can be more easily done in this area than any other. The right balance is difficult to strike. In relation to the mentally disabled and 'autistic', for example, an attempt to be sympathetic can readily lead to an author employing the 'beautiful but dumb' stereotype. On the other hand, attempts at realism can produce the equally unhelpful approach which confirms the stereotypal association between low intelligence or emotional impairment and an ugly appearance.

Fanta Shyer in *Welcome Home, Jellybean* seems to hit the right note:

'Sometimes between words Gerri forgets to close her mouth and just leaves it open. That's when she looks all wrong and funny; otherwise when her hair is combed right, she looks pretty much like every other kid and a lot prettier than some of the girls in my class. Her top teeth are crooked, but mine were too, until I got braces.' (p. 16)

Gerri has her own peculiarities, but then most children do, and when it really comes down to it there is not that much difference between her looks and anyone else's. Although her peculiarities are recognised, the author's description — 'she looks all wrong and funny' — has a humorous edge but avoids cynicism. Similar approaches are adopted in Wrightson's *I Own the Racecourse* and Slepian's *The Alfred Summer*, whereas in Spence's descriptions of Carl in *The October Child*, and Brown's of Debbie in *The Siblings* there is too much emphasis on the exceptional beauty of the disabled children in question.

Secondly, the behaviour of the disabled child should be described in a way which accurately reflects the kind of behaviour that would be expected of a child with that disability. Although this is important, I do not agree that any inaccuracy here should mean the immediate withdrawal of the book. It may have other strengths which compensate for the error. For instance, the speech patterns of Danny Price in Kemp's *The Turbulent Term of Tyke Tiler* may not consistently reflect his supposed defect, but one would not reject this deeply humane book on these grounds alone.

Thirdly, even when the author is not primarily concerned with conveying a sense of the 'inner world' of the disabled character, it seems important to acknowledge that the behaviour described usually has a meaning for the person emitting it. Again, this is an issue to which one would expect authors writing about mentally disabled characters to be especially sensitive. In Byars' *The Summer of the Swans* the subjectivity of the child is conveyed by devoting whole chapters to descriptions of his thoughts, feelings, fears and anxieties as he experiences them.

Fourthly, one should consider whether the book relies for its effect on a romanticised view of 'handicap'. There are two contrasting stereotypes which are typical of this view. The first is one which overestimates the talents of a disabled child. For example, the child might be portrayed as achieving goals which would be impossible for someone in his or her condition, as when an autistic child who loves music learns to play the Brahms violin concerto, or when a mentally disabled child suddenly becomes more intelligent in a crisis situation. The theme of 'unlocking' the talent of the disabled child is pervasive in Victorian literature and in some modern literature. It reflects the wishful thinking of many parents of seriously disabled children who want to believe that there is a great but hidden potential within their child. Equally romantic but in the reverse direction is the underestimation of the talents of disabled children. Such children are kindly and charitable in a saintly way, and are portrayed as 'victims', but they are not given to being particularly active, creative or intelligent. A book which avoids both these traps is Wrightson's *I Own the Racecourse*. Andy, a slow-learning boy who is the hero of the story is certainly active and shows plenty of initiative, but there are clearly defined boundaries to his achievements which bring him down to earth, albeit gently and with dignity.

In general, the problem with stereotypes is that even if they are 'favourable' (e.g. as when the child is portrayed as a 'virtuous victim') they are still counterproductive if the aim is to present disabled children as rounded characters interacting with others with diverse possibilities for psychological and social outcomes. A stereotype is a trap because it restricts the characterisation to one dominant social identity. It is not that being considered a 'virtuous victim' or a 'suffering angel' is undesirable in itself, but if this is all one is, then it is as dehumanising as being looked upon as having 'bad blood' or as being 'possessed'. Disabled children should be portrayed as persons, warts an' all, with a range of human characteristics. Even the stereotype of the disabled person always being 'brave' is objectionable, because for many disabled persons it is a distortion of reality. Perhaps bravery is involved, but the hard work of making an adjustment may be done out of plain necessity — in other words, a normally human as opposed to superhuman endeavour. Allan Sutherland's (1981) opinion of this stereotype is worth quoting.

A stereotype that we particularly resent is the one that says how brave we are. We find ourselves continually being put in to the same position as the child who squirms with embarrassment as a fond parent boasts about achievements that she takes no particular interest in herself. We are not remotely as obsessed with our disabilities as many able-bodied people obviously assume, we have our own lives to lead and we get on with leading them. (p. 67)

One's impression is that stereotypes of the most distasteful kind are rare in children's fiction, but they do surface occasionally as in *The Siblings*, particularly when the author attempts to capture the interest of older readers by highlighting the extremes of disability and the extremes of behaviour associated with them. Of course, there is nothing objectionable about portraying the severity of disability and the disruptive effects this may have on family life and social life generally. Often, people unfamiliar with disability just do not know of the traumas involved in bringing up a child with severe learning or communication difficulties, or one who is severely physically handicapped, and if a story makes them aware of this then all well and good. But it is possible to write about severe disability in such a way that the 'horror' of it all is the main hook. The disabled child is portrayed as a sinister figure, not possessed by the devil exactly, but behaving so outrageously and anti-socially that other people feel threatened and even frightened. The author's intention appears to be to write a horror story rather than to genuinely explore attitudes towards disability.

How Does the Book Deal with Prejudice, Discrimination and Role-stereotyping in Society Generally?

It is important to remain alert to the possibility that although the disabled character is portrayed satisfactorily, the book as a whole includes portraits of other characters and situations which reinforce divisions in society which are potentially equally damaging to the cause of the disabled. I have included some reference to this point in most chapters, but it is elaborated upon mainly in Chapter 4 in discussion on the theme of 'friendships across the divide'. The divide referred to is not only that between the 'normal' and 'disabled' but also that created by social class, sex and racial discrimination.

I have argued that there is little sense in portraying the 'hooligans' and 'bullies', for example, who threaten a disabled child or his or her sibling, as always lower-working-class in terms of social background. Such characters may come from this background, but not always. It is precisely these divisions, reinforced by such stereotyping and in inter-action with each other and other factors, which help to perpetuate discrimination against the disabled in the first instance. In the case of lower-working-class youth, confining them to the lowest rung of a hierarchically organised society, treating them as deviants in the media, making them unemployed and taking away their dignity is hardly likely to create personalities who will respond to exhortations from educators that they should be sympathetic towards the disabled. The truly wonderful thing is that many of them are sympathetic despite their oppression.

I am suggesting that a book which reinforces the class divisions of our society is inevitably counterproductive if the aim is to further understanding of the need to integrate children with disabilities. Beresford's *The Four of Us*, Wilson's *A Friendship of Equals* and Allan's *The Flash Children* each in its different way reflects the author's lack of sensitivity to this issue. Marshall's *I Can Jump Puddles*, despite obvious weaknesses in relation to the male/female divide, provides the best illustration of the support for the disabled from those at the bottom of society's heap, whereas Allan's *The View Beyond My Father* contains a blind girl's criticisms of the class society she lives in.

A similar point can be made about stereotypes derived from a sexist view of male/female relationships. If the mother is always portrayed as the key figure in caring for a disabled child to the exclusion of father, then this can only reinforce the conventional view of a woman's role. The consequence is that such children are deprived of father's attention because his opting-out is legitimated. Stereotypes of boy/girl relationships which buttress sexual divisions are also counterproductive for similar reasons.

In general, portraits of the community context in which the action takes place have to be just as carefully examined as those of the disabled children themselves and their immediate families. Families do not exist in splendid isolation. They interact with others outside the home — friends, neighbours, relatives, professionals, etc. Not all neighbours bang on walls, not all social workers are misguided, not all nurses are angels, and not all children who go around in gangs are bullies.

How Does the Book Deal with Official Labelling and Special Provision?

Where the author uses an official label we would expect this to be used correctly. Thus, a child should not be described as 'mentally handicapped' where 'having mild learning difficulties' would be more appropriate. Similarly, we would expect the author to have done his homework on the nature and effects of various 'treatments'. Thus, it is erroneous to suggest, for example, that drugs can somehow cure mental handicap, or that surgery can make a cerebral-palsied child physically normal, or that psychotherapy can instantly 'cure' severe emotional disorders.

But probably the best approach is to adopt a stance which is critical of official labelling and the 'treatment' orientation as such. It should be remembered that a central guiding notion of the Warnock Report was that the distinction between two groups of children — the handicapped and the non-handicapped — should be broken down (in fact, as I indicated earlier, the Report was not consistent on this point), and to this end it recommended that the statutory categorisation of handicap be abolished and replaced by detailed descriptions of special educational needs (para. 3.25). One of the reasons given for this recommendation was that this distinction between the groups led to labelling and the labels tended to stick *and* be stigmatising. I would argue that the most counterproductive form of labelling in terms of stickability and stigmatisation is that involving medical terminology, e.g. 'phobia', 'dyslexia', 'disorder', and it was because of their uncritical use of such terms that I had misgivings about Mildiner's and House's *The Gates* and Kennemore's *Wall of Words*.

Another aspect which requires careful handling is special provision. In some of the books discussed placement in a special school is treated unproblematically as an appropriate educational arrangement for the child concerned, e.g. Robinson's *David in Silence*, Lamplugh's *Sean's Leap*, Mildiner's and House's *The Gates*. Others, however, are more critical of this practice, e.g. Allan's *The Flash Children*. Other institutions that figure in these books are the residential training centre, e.g. Shyer's *Welcome Home, Jellybean*, the hospital, e.g. Jones's *The View from the Window*, the assessment centre, e.g. Ashley's *Dodgem* and the residential nursing home, e.g. Sallis's *Sweet Frannie*. All the books mentioned here probe the rhetoric of care and examine the practices in the institution concerned. Jones in particular provides a most lucid account of a disabled person's attempts to come to terms with the rules and regulations of institutional life, and the different views of the regime.

How Does the Book Deal with Social and Psychological Change in Childhood and Adolescence?

This may not seem a terribly relevant issue to the reader, but I would argue that in some ways it is the most crucial. At several points I have referred to an author's conventional approach to development in childhood and adolescence − an adaptational model where the youngster is expected to adapt to a reality as defined by adults, i.e. adapt to the *status quo*. As in Schneider's *If Only I Could Walk*, the young persons' 'mistakes' are due largely to their not being in touch with reality as they struggle for identity in the adult world. Fortunately, there is usually an adult or an older sibling or friend to hand to explain things to them. They end up being more mature, more sure of themselves, and realising what fools they had been in the past.

Such a model leaves out two vital considerations: (a) that young persons may not choose to adapt but might wish to create their own reality, and, indeed, often do and (b) that adults may not be solid members of a stable society but volatile members of a relatively unstable society, who are in the process themselves of asking questions about the nature of the society in which they live.

My argument is that unless these two points are taken into account, then certain important options for the young person are not being explored in the text which, as a consequence, is reduced in its scope for suggesting alternative modes of existence for the disabled. In short, the book merely confirms the kinds of attitudes and beliefs which are indirectly at the root of much prejudice and discrimination against them. I am thinking, for example, of the emphasis amongst youth in our culture on the importance of physical attractiveness as commercially defined, and the relationship between this and a young person's perception of his or her position in the marriage market. It is when trying to conform to such values that young disabled people feel most oppressed.

Using the Literature

Teachers will know of several ways that these books can be used in schools, but I want to focus on a few aspects of teaching approaches which seem to me to be the most relevant in terms of the general tenor of the discussion in this book. One obvious approach is to select passages from a book which highlight particular points about the disability. They could involve a description of the disability or explanations as to its cause or an exploration of the feelings of disabled persons themselves – and then these extracts used to initiate a discussion on the issues involved. The class are then required to do a project on, say, the physically handicapped. Physically handicapped adults are invited to the school to talk to the class. The pupils write to the local authority to ask what provision is made for people with this disability. There may be some experiential learning sessions (e.g. playing hockey in wheelchairs or trying to move about without using the legs) or role-playing in addition to the more usual activities of looking up information in the library and collecting newspaper items.

This approach is perfectly valid, but there is a tendency in such project work for the fictional literature to play at best a minimal supporting role and at worst to be regarded as the 'chore' academic exercise amongst a relatively more stimulating series of activities. In either case, the literature's potential is clearly not being exploited to the full. The book is not read as a complete text, but is 'pillaged' for what it says about a particular aspect of the experience of handicap. Now the passages chosen may be interesting and stimulate project work, but I would argue, and I think many teachers would agree, that this is only one way to go about teaching the topic and that an alternative approach – and one which makes better use of the fiction – is to explore the issues via an immersion in the world of the novel concerned.

To some this might seem a rather bookish approach, or even one overly influenced by 'Eng. Lit.' imperialism! I would respond by declaring no vested interest, and, more importantly, by asserting that although clearly novels do have their 'best bits' these cannot really be appreciated without taking a reasonably close look at the novel as a whole. It is a commonplace that much of the emotional impact of a book derives from the reader following the narrative through from beginning to end – anticipating the story's development, reacting to and reconstructing the characters, thinking and feeling oneself into the author's secondary world, and going back over passages to obtain a deeper understanding of them. The approach to teaching the book which takes this into account is primarily concerned with teaching the child how to read the book.

This can lead to an about-face of the project method briefly outlined above. Instead of passages from novels being used to introduce the topic, experimental sessions and other activities are used as a lead into reading the book and as an aid to understanding it in greater depth. Of course, I make this point only to demonstrate the other side of the coin, so to speak. In reality, the process is dialectical and the different approaches are interdependent, from experience to book, from book to experience.

I shall now provide an illustration of a teaching approach to *Welcome Home, Jellybean*. It seems to me that the process begins with self-analysis on the part of the teacher, who knows the book is about a mentally handicapped child. Has the teacher ever taught such a child? What are the teacher's feelings about such children? How much does the teacher know about mental handicap? Teachers should explore their own reactions to the book, and attempt to make explicit their thoughts and feelings about it by writing reviews. Some teachers may feel that this point hardly needs to be made it is so obvious, but it is worth stressing here because of the nature of the subject matter. Many people who are otherwise caring and sympathetic towards children with problems have a block when it comes to the mentally handicapped. It is worth checking on one's own attitude here by visiting a special school and spending a couple of hours in the company of the children there, or if this is not possible by visiting the home of a friend or neighbour who has such a child.

The second step might be to carry out a similar exercise with the pupils. There are several possibilities. Visits to special schools could be arranged, but one has to be careful not to confirm the idea that these children usually require segregated provision. A better approach would be to invite the parents or the older sibling(s) of a mentally disabled child to the school to discuss life at home – a video recording might be useful here. Talks from visiting professionals could also be considered. This initial period of sensitisation could also involve drama work, group discussion and project-type activities, but perhaps these are best left to a later stage.

The next two steps are what Cheetham (1982) describes as the basic phase and the project phase. The first of these involves reading the book to the class, virtually straight through with some clarification of certain aspects when the need arises. For instance, the teacher might have to explain why Geraldine spoke in the way she did. Also the first two chapters about life in the training centre might require some explanation. Children might not understand why she had been placed there in the first place if it was such a bad experience for her. A number of points might generate spontaneous discussion, but in general an attempt should be made to read the book through for the pure enjoyment of it. It is certainly a book that is suitable for reading aloud to the class. The style is simple and lively, there is plenty of humour and irony, the language is light and jokey, and none of the chapters is more than a few pages long. (I have in mind a top junior or early secondary mixed-ability class.)

In the project phase the emphasis is on creative activities inspired by the story, and the novel is used as a kind of reference book. This latter point is crucial. The book is not just read and put back on the shelf but is constantly returned to, and certain passages may be read several times. The creative work itself is carried out away from the pages, so to speak, but the products of this work in terms of further questions raised and insights generated react back on the reading experience — broadening and deepening the child's understanding of the book. This transaction between reader and book is encouraged and extended during this phase.

The teacher's role is clearly to facilitate this transaction, and might be to suggest a number of themes which the children could explore in group discussion or written work. The following list is not comprehensive, but gives an indication of some of the main themes.

(1) Life away from home in residential institutions, e.g. children could draw on their experiences of going into hospital (or those of a sibling or a friend).

(2) Feelings about brother and/or sisters, e.g. jealousy, protectiveness, annoyance, anger, frustration, feeling constrained.

(3) Embarrassment, e.g. particularly when this involves an interfering sibling.

(4) Facing up to conflict between parents.

(5) Trying to make teachers understand the problems you have at home, e.g. explaining to teachers why homework is difficult to do.

(6) Trying to communicate with someone who has a learning difficulty.

(7) Coping with hostile neighbours, e.g. the noise problem.

(8) Bullying.

Art work might not seem an appropriate medium for the thoughts and feelings generated by this particular book, but in fact there is plenty of scope for creative processes here. The teacher might be able to see in the way the characters are drawn or painted the child's changing perception of mental handicap. Is Geraldine's appearance, for example, intentionally distorted by the child therefore suggesting, perhaps, the mental handicap is associated with physical deformity? If not, how is her mental handicap conveyed visually? The child can be referred back to the text before, during or after the drawing or painting session, and by doing so the teacher can raise questions for the child about attitudes and emotions. Any discrepancy between information in the text and visual portrayal may be revealing of the child's continuing misunderstanding of what the author is trying to say. The same point can be made about the characters in the rest of the family and the portrayal of family relationships. Is the father portrayed as living away from home (in the book he leaves home to live in a flat)? How is mother drawn or painted? Is there any suggestion of the effects of having to look after Geraldine, e.g. does she look tired? In a sketch of the family group, how are they oriented towards each other, e.g. who is closest to Geraldine? Of course, one must be careful not to overinterpret pictures, and an in-depth psychological diagnosis is not what I am suggesting. It is really a question of using one or two ideas which may have been sparked off by the art work as yet another way of entering the text.

Drama work also provides an indication of a child's attitude, as well as being a learning experience in itself. I would see this as having various functions, but one of the most useful would be in establishing a basis for a more critical approach to the book. As I have pointed out, although this novel provides some excellent insights into the experience of living with a mentally handicapped child, it can be faulted for using the traditional stereotype of the 'bullies from off the housing estate' in the form of Beefy and his cronies. Geraldine's family are middle class, and were it not for her arrival on the scene Neil would have attended a private school. Neil is clearly too preoccupied with his own survival to have much time or inclination to develop an understanding of Beefy and his predicament, but if the criteria of evaluation outlined earlier are to be taken seriously than some indication of Beefy as victim as well as persecutor is necessary. In so doing the expression of alternative views of what one can expect from children who live on 'housing estates' might be forthcoming — how they are not all hostile to disabled people, and can be caring and supportive. For example, a child might be asked to play Beefy and put his side of the story and perhaps even that of his cronies. Situations can be created which do not even occur in the novel. Some notion of the underlying parameters or subtext of the book can be generated by this type of activity. In this way, sympathies for Neil and Geraldine can be contextualised and broadened to include others who do not have obvious problems, but may react the way they do because they also feel rejected by society. The overall aim is to arrive at some appreciation of the interconnectedness of human problems.

Finally, to round off this section, a few comments are necessary on the audience for whom these books are intended. For the most part I have in mind children and young persons in mainstream classes in the ordinary school, and I have assumed that children with disabilities may themselves be present in such classes. Clearly, if a child in the class has the disability which is being portrayed in the story this is a delicate situation and one that will need carefully handling by the teacher, who may feel that a book which was about a disability other than the one present should be selected. On the other hand, the teacher may feel that in the context of particular classroom relationships great benefits could be derived from children with disabilities making observations on the text which assisted their peers' interpretation of the story or raised questions which the book either ignored or dealt with poorly. It would also give such children an opportunity to express their feelings to the group.

However, too much should not be made of the 'privileged' position of the child with the disability in this respect because clearly capacity for insight into their own psychologies can vary considerably from child to child. It is also important to remember that *all* children should be encouraged to develop a personal response to the book, and this may be just as illuminating for the child with the disability as for the rest of the class. In fact, this is one of the great strengths of fiction – it demands of all children that they project into an imaginary world, whether the characters are superficially like them in some way or not, and in the process of doing so all kinds of responses are possible. It is even possible to imagine a non-disabled child having a greater affinity to a disabled hero or heroine than a child with the same disability as this character, simply because in the final analysis it is personality and action in a story context which is the interest hook rather than the disability itself.

Conclusion

My primary concern in this book has been to discuss how disability is portrayed in modern children's fiction with a view to suggesting criteria that the teacher might employ when selecting books on the topic. The themes selected carry with them assumptions about which issues should be salient for the teacher. Thus, the emphasis has been on 'human relationships' rather than on technical information about disability, and within that area I have been concerned with the unique interactive context of each book, involving children with disabilities, their siblings, friends, parents and other adults. The discussion has been mainly about how the fiction deals with these relationships and the evaluative criteria evolved derive from a consideration of this feature in relation to integrationist ideals.

Many of the arguments presented have clear implications for action research and I hope that teachers and others will feel inclined to pursue matters further in this field. The following are suggested as useful points of departure:

(1) In the secondary school English teachers and Special Needs (e.g. Remedial) teachers could share experiences of using books in this genre.

(2) These two groups could then perhaps initiate a discussion in their schools on how disability is dealt with in the formal and informal curriculum.

(3) This discussion could take place in the context of a general concern to change curricula and establish new priorities. The question might be asked: What place would teaching about disabilities have in a revamped common curriculum?

(4) A similar process might take place in the primary school, except that all teachers would be involved from the start.

(5) An important consideration in all discussions would be how curriculum development in this area might relate to ongoing integration programmes.

(6) At the level of classroom practice, individual teachers could carry out small-scale empirical studies monitoring the children's responses to books and noting any changes in attitude or behaviour. In the context of mixed-ability grouping it would be interesting to assess the contribution of sensitisation through fiction to the ongoing aim of fostering co-operation and mutual assistance in learning tasks amongst pupils.

GLOSSARY

The following terms are explained in the hope that a wide range of readers will be able to appreciate the descriptions and arguments in this book. Some terms are likely to be familiar to British, but not to American readers. Others will be very familiar to special education teachers for example, but less so, to students of children's literature who have less contact with disabled children.

A-levels: public examination for academically oriented pupils usually taken at 18+, after O-levels. (A = advanced, O = ordinary level.)

Aggro: slang term meaning aggression and violence.

Assessment centre: an establishment for the observation and assessment of children and adolescents referred by the courts.

Autism: condition about which there is controversy, but which is usually characterised by absence of emotional relationships, lack of speech and serious problems of relating to others.

BBC: British Broadcasting Corporation. 'BBC-type' speech is often held up as a 'correct' form of pronunciation.

Bobby: popular word for a British policeman.

Down's Syndrome: often termed 'Down Syndrome' in the US. Previously called mongolism. It is characterised by varying degrees of mental retardation and is usually due to an extra chromosome 21.

Education Act 1981: the central law governing special education in England and Wales.

Greengrocery: name for a shop which sells only fruit and vegetables.

Housing estate: an area set aside for residential housing only.

Infant school: school for children between the ages of five and seven.

Integration: equivalent to mainstreaming, but used in this book to include other forms of integration e.g. racial.

Joint Committee 1980: an organ of the Joint Council for the Education of Handicapped Children; a professional grouping.

Junior school: school for children between the ages of seven and eleven.

Local authority (local education authority): the local organ of government responsible for educational provision.

Middle school: school for children between the ages of eight and twelve, or nine and thirteen, or ten and thirteen, depending on local arrangements. The first school/middle school is an alternative organisation of primary education to the infant school/junior school, but is not available in all areas.

O-Levels: 16+ public examinations, for academically-oriented pupils. Some, but not all, will then move on to take A-levels.

Primary school: combined infant and junior school.

Secondary school: for age range eleven to sixteen, compulsory; sixteen to nineteen voluntary.

Spina bifida: congential malformation of the spinal cord, the covering of the cord and the nearby vertebrae.

Subnormality hospital: residential institution for the mentally handicapped or retarded.

Tied cottage: a cottage (house) tied to a job which must be vacated when employment ceases.

Twigs: used as a verb this means to understand or to suddenly realise the true meaning of someone's words, e.g. at last he twigged the joke.

Warnock Report: a government initiated report into the education of handicapped children and young people which reported in 1978 (see Preface).

REFERENCES

List A: Children's Novels

Allan, M.E. (1978) *The View Beyond My Father*, London, Abelard-Schuman/ New York, Dodd
—— (1979) *The Flash Children*, London, Hamlyn (first published Brockhampton Press, 1975)/New York, Dodd
Althea (1983) *I Have Diabetes*, Cambridge, Dinosaur Publications
—— (1983) *I Use a Wheelchair*, Cambridge, Dinosaur Publications
Ashley, B. (1983) *Dodgem*, Harmondsworth, Puffin Books (first published 1981)/ 1982, New York, Franklin Watts
Beckman, G. (1981) *Nineteen Is Too Young To Die*, London, Macmillan (first published 1971)/New York, Harcourt Brace
Beresford, E. (1981) *The Four of Us*, London, Hutchinson
Bloom, F. (1977) *The Boy Who Couldn't Hear*, London, The Bodley Head/Topsfield, Massachusetts, Merrimack Book Services
Brown, R. (1975) *The Siblings*, London, Abelard-Schuman (also published as *Find Debbie*, 1979, Penguin)/1976, Boston, Houghton Mifflin
Byars, B. (1980) *The Summer of the Swans*, London, Scholastic Publications Ltd (first published 1970, New York, Viking Press Inc.)
Chapman, K. (1982) *Suzy*, London, The Bodley Head
Cleaver, V. and B. (1977) *The Mimosa Tree*, Oxford UP (first published 1970, Harper and Row, New York)
Cookson, C. (1982) *Our John Willie*, London, Piccolo (first published MacDonald & Co., 1974)/1975, New York, New American Library
DeJong, M. (1968) *Journey from Peppermint Street*, London, Lutterworth Press/ 1974, New York, Harper
—— (1981) *The Wheel on the School*, Harmondsworth, Puffin (first published 1954, New York, Harper)
Edwards, M. (1969) *A Wind is Blowing*, London, Collins
Fanshawe, E. (1975) *Rachel*, London, The Bodley Head/Scarsdale, New York, Bradbury
Haigh, S. (1975) *Watch for the Ghost*, London, Methuen
Hoy, L. (1981) *Your Friend, Rebecca*, London, Sydney, Toronto, The Bodley Head
Jones, C. (1978) *The View from The Window*, London, Andre Deutsch
Kata, E. (1982) *A Patch of Blue*, Harmondsworth, Penguin (first published M. Joseph, 1961)/1975, New York, Macmillan, Popular Library Inc.
Keats, E.J. (1975) *Apt. 3*, London, Hamish Hamilton/New York, Macmillan
Kemp, G. (1981) *Gowie Corby Plays Chicken*, Harmondsworth, Puffin (first published Faber & Faber, 1979)
—— (1981) *The Turbulent Term of Tyke Tiler*, Harmondsworth, Puffin (first published Faber & Faber, 1977)
Kennemore, T. (1983) *Wall of Words*, London, Faber & Faber

Kerr, M.E. (1973) *Dinky Hocker Shoots Smack*, London, Gollancz/1972, New York, Harper & Row
Lamplugh, L. (1979) *Sean's Leap*, London, Deutsch
Marshall, A. (1983) *I Can Jump Puddles*, Harmondsworth, Puffin (first published in Australia, 1955)
Marshall, M. (1983) *Mike*, London, The Bodley Head/Topsfield, Massachusetts, Merrimack Book Services
Mildiner, L. and House, B. (1974) *The Gates*, London, Centreprise Publishing Project
Peter, D. (1977) *Claire and Emma*, London, A. & C. Black/New York, Harper & Row
Petersen, P. (1976) *Sally Can't See*, London, A. & C. Black
Robinson, V. (1965) *David in Silence*, London, Deutsch/1966, Philadelphia, Lippincott
Rodowsky, C.F. (1976) *What About Me?* New York & London, Franklin Watts 1978, New York, Dell
Sallis, S. (1983) *Sweet Frannie*, Harmondsworth, Puffin (first published Heinemann, 1981)
Schneider, M. (1978) *If Only I Could Walk*, London, Heinemann
Shyer, M.F. (1982) *Welcome Home, Jellybean*, London, Granada (first published 1978, New York, Charles Scribner & Sons)
Slepian, J. (1980) *The Alfred Summer*, New York, Macmillan
Snell, N. (1981) *Jane Has Asthma*, London, Hamish Hamilton/Distributed in USA: North Pomfret, Vermont, David & Charles
Spence, E. (1976) *The October Child*, London, Oxford University Press
Southall, I. (1981) *Let the Balloon Go*, Harmondsworth, Puffin (first published, 1968, London, Methuen)/1969, New York, St Martin's Press
Taylor, T. (1981) *The Cay*, Harmondsworth, Puffin (first published 1969, New York, Doubleday)
Walsh, J.P. (1975) *Goldengrove*, London, Macmillan (first published 1972, New York, Farrat, Straus & Giroux)
—— (1976) *Unleaving*, London, Macmillan/1977, New York, Avon Books
White, P. (1978) *Janet at School*, London, Adam & Charles Black/New York, Harper & Row
Wilson, G. (1981) *A Friendship of Equals*, London & Boston, Faber & Faber
Wilson, P.M. and Irvine, S. (1983) *If You Knew Nicky*, London, Angus & Robertson
Wrightson, P. (1980) *I Own the Racecourse*, Harmondsworth, Puffin (first published 1968, London, Hutchinson)/1968, New York, Harcourt Brace

List B: Other References

Baskin, B.H. and Harris, K.H. (1977) *Notes from a Different Drummer*, New York, R.R. Bowker Co.
Bettelheim, B. and Zelan, K. (1981) 'Why Children Don't Like to Read', *Atlantic Monthly*, November
Booth, T. (1982) *Handicap Is Social*, Milton Keynes, The Open University Press
——, Potts, P. and Swann, W. (1982) *Research and Progress in Special Education*, Milton Keynes, The Open University Press
Campling, J. (1981) *Images of Ourselves: Women with Disabilities Talking*, London,

References   171

Henley & Boston, Routledge & Kegan Paul

Cheetham, J. (1982) 'Quarries in the Primary School', in M. Hoffman, R. Jeffcoate, J. Maybin and N. Mercer, *Children, Language and Literature*, Milton Keynes, The Open University Press

Cianciolo, P. (1978) in G. Fox and G. Hammond, *Responses to Children's Literature*, K.G. Saur/US, distributor: Hamden, CT, Shoe String Press, pp. 102–8

Darling, R.B. (1979) *Families Against Society: A Study of Reactions to Children with Birth Defects*, Beverley Hills, Calif., Sage Publications

Department of Education and Science (1978) *Special Educational Needs* (the Warnock Report), London, HMSO

Dixon, B. (1977) *Catching Them Young: Sex, Race and Class in Children's Fiction*, London, Pluto Press

Fox, G. (1971) 'Growth and Masquerade: A Theme in the Novels of Ivan Southall', *Children's Literature in Education*, 6, 49–64

Furneaux, B. (1981) *The Special Child*, Harmondsworth, Penguin (3rd edn)

Galloway, D.M. and Goodwin, C. (1979) *Educating Slow Learning and Maladjusted Children: Integration or Segregation*, New York & London, Longman

Gath, A. (1978) *Down's Syndrome and the Family: the Early Years*, New York & London, Academic Press

Goffman, E. (1971) *The Presentation of Self in Everyday Life*, Harmondsworth, Penguin/1973, New York, The Overlook Press

Hargreaves, D.H. (1982) *The Challenge for the Comprehensive School*, London & Boston, Routledge & Kegan Paul

——, Hestor, S. and Mellor, F. (1975) *Deviance in Classrooms*, London & Boston, Routledge & Kegan Paul

Hegarty, S. and Pocklington, K. (1981) *Educating Pupils with Special Needs in the Ordinary School*, Slough, NFER-Nelson/Atlantic Highlands, NJ, Humanities Press

Henry, J. (1963) *Culture Against Man*, Harmondsworth, Penguin, 1965, NY, Random

Hopkins, C.J. (1982) 'Representation of the Handicapped in Basal Readers', in *Reading Teacher*, vol. 36, no. 1, 30–2

Joint Council for the Education of Handicapped Children (1980) *Integration or Segregation? A False Alternative*, London, JCEHC

Kahn, J. and Nursten, J. (1968) *Unwillingly to School*, Oxford and London, Pergamon

Kesey, K. (1973) *One Flew Over the Cuckoo's Nest*, London, Picador-Pan, 1977, NY, Penguin

Lash, J.P. (1980) *Helen and Teacher*, Harmondsworth, Penguin

Leach, D.J. and Raybould, E.C. (1977) *Learning and Behaviour Difficulties in School*, London, Open Books/Atlantic Highlands, NJ, Humanities Press

Mehta, V. (ed.) (1978) *Face to Face*, New York, Oxford University Press

Meighan, R. (1981) *A Sociology of Educating*, London, Holt, Rinehart & Winston

Newson, E. and Hipgrave, T. (1982) *Getting Through to Your Handicapped Child*, Cambridge, Cambridge University Press

Nightingale, C. (1974) 'What Katy Didn't Do', *Spare Rib*, February

Potter, J., Stringer, P. and Wetherell, M. (1984) *Social Texts and Context*, London & Boston, Routledge & Kegan Paul

Quicke, J.C. (1975) 'Humanistic Psychology and Educational Objectives in Schools for the Maladjusted', in *Therapeutic Education*, vol. 3, no. 2, 18–23

―――― (1981) 'Special Educational Needs and the Comprehensive Principle: Some Implications of Ideological Critique', *Remedial Education*, vol. 16, no. 2, 61–7

―――― (1982) *The Cautious Expert*, Milton Keynes, The Open University Press

―――― (1984) 'The Role of the Educational Psychologist in the Post-Warnock Era', in L. Barton and S. Tomlinson (eds), *Special Education and Social Interests*, London, Croom Helm/New York, Nichols

Roe, M. (1978) 'Medical and Psychological Concepts of Problem Behaviour', in B. Gillham, *Reconstructing Educational Psychology*, London, Croom Helm/ US Distributor: Dover, NH, Longwood

Rogers, C.R. (1951) *Client-centred Therapy*, Boston, Mass., Houghton Mifflin

Rosser, E. and Harré, R. (1976) 'The Meaning of "Trouble" ', in M. Hammersley and P. Woods, *The Process of Schooling*, London, Henley & Boston, Routledge & Kegan Paul, Milton Keynes, The Open University Press

Ryan, J. and Thomas, F. (1980) *The Politics of Mental Handicap*, Harmondsworth, Penguin

Sedgwick, P. (1972) 'R.D. Laing: Self, Symptom and Society', in P. Boyers and R. Orrill (eds), *Laing and Anti-Psychiatry*, Harmondsworth, Penguin/1974, New York, Octagon Books

Shearer, A. (1981) *Disability: Whose Handicap?* Oxford, Basil Blackwell

Sutherland, A.T. (1981) *Disabled We Stand*, London, Souvenir Press, New York, State Mutual Books

Thomas, D. (1982) *The Experience of Handicap*, London & New York, Methuen

Tomlinson, S. (1981) *Educational Subnormality: A Study of Decision Making*, London & Boston, Routledge & Kegan Paul

Tringo, J.L. (1970) 'The Hierarchy of Preference Towards Disability Groups', *Journal of Special Education*, vol. 4, no. 3, 295

Wallace, M. and Robson, M. (1977) *On Giants Shoulders*, London, Corgi

Weinberg, L.A. (1981) 'The Problem of Defending Equal Rights for the Handicapped', *Educational Theory*, vol. 31, no. 2, 177–87

Willis, P. (1977) *Learning to Labour*, Farnborough, Saxon House/1981, New York, Columbia University Press

Woods, P. (ed.) (1980) *Pupil Strategies*, London, Croom Helm/US distributor: Dover, NH, Longwood

Worpole, K. (1975) ' "The Gates": Writing Within the Community', in *Children's Literature in Education, 17*, 76–87

Zaretsky, E. (1976) *Capitalism, the Family and Personal Life*, London, Pluto Press/New York, Harper & Row

INDEX

adolescence 22, 104, 116, 118–20, 160; adaptation model of 22, 116, 120; stage of development 104
Alfred Summer, The 72–5, 76, 77, 155, 168
Allan, M.E. 39, 167
Althea 143, 145, 169
altruism 41
anti-psychiatry 43
Apt. 3 140, 169
art 164
Ashley, B. 122, 169
asthma 136–7
Australia 54, 55
autistic 29, 30, 148, 155; *see also* non-communicating
autobiographical 54

Baskin, B.H. 6, 170
Beckman, G. 111, 169
behaviour problems 66; *see also* maladjusted, truancy
Beresford, E. 60, 169
Berg, L. 85
Bettelheim, B. 140, 170
blind 39–43, 100, 101, 126–30, 143; blindness in adolescence 39–43; blindness in adults 126–30; *see also* partially sighted
Bloom, F. 137, 169
Booth, T. 4, 26
Boy Who Couldn't Hear, The 137, 138, 169
Brown, R. 33, 169
bully 57, 125, 158
Byars, B. 27, 169

catharsis 90, 92, 94
Cay, The 65–6, 170
cerebral palsy 49, 72–5
Chapman, E. 141, 169
Cheetham, J. 162, 171
Cianciolo, P. 151, 171
class 18, 56, 60, 61, 62, 63–5, 84, 117, 126, 158; class system 63–5; 'estate people' 61; ruling

class 63; working class 60, 62, 65, 84, 126
Cleaver, B. 129, 169
Cleaver, V. 129, 169
community 48, 59, 60, 78, 130, 159
compassion 56, 68·
comprehensive school 1–2, 85, 90
contradictions 37
Cookson, C. 64, 169
Cooper, D. 43

Darling, R.B. 14, 171
David in Silence 69–72, 77, 159, 170
deaf 64, 69–72 *passim*, 130, 137, 138, 140; deafness in adults 130, 137, 138; deafness in children 69–72, 140
death 111, 121
De Jong, M. 130, 169
depression 110
diabetes 145, 146
Dinky Hocker Shoots Smack 43–9, 169
disabled adults Chapter 8
discrimination 2, 145, 151, 158–9, 160; *see also* class, race, sexism
Dixon, B. 65
doctor 49, 149; *see also* medical model
Dodgem 122–6, 128, 129, 134, 160, 169
do-gooder 77–8, 109
domination 38, 116
double blind 43–9 *passim*
Down's syndrome 23–7 *passim*
drama 93, 94, 164
dyslexia 80–4 *passim*

Education Act (1981) 1
education welfare officer 126
Edwards, M. 100, 169
egocentricity 39, 93
élitism 26
emancipation 42
emotional disturbance (difficulties) Chapter 6, 122–6
enuresis 149

173